THE
BOOK OF
DISTINGUISHED
AMERICAN
WOMEN

VINCENT WILSON, JR.

*Cover Design
by James Cavender*

American History Research Associates
Brookeville, Maryland

Printed in the United States of America
by
R.R. Donnelley & Sons Company
Crawfordsville, Indiana

Composition by Graphica, Inc.,
Lanham, Maryland

LIBRARY OF CONGRESS CARD NO. 83-71544
ISBN 0-910086-05-2

American History Research Associates

BOX 140, BROOKVILLE, MARYLAND

CONTENTS

ADVISORY GROUP OF SCHOLARS

The fifty* American women whose biographies appear in this book were selected by the author with the very considerable assistance of an Advisory Group of Scholars, specialists in the field of women's studies and the role of women in American History.

Only native-born Americans were considered, and, as with most biographical dictionaries, no living persons were considered. The size and format of the book dictated the number of subjects.

Members of the Advisory Group

Ms. Edith Mayo
Chief, Division of Political History
The National Museum of American History
The Smithsonian Institution

Dr. Evelyn Pugh
Professor of History
George Mason University

Ms. Sarah Pritchard
Reference Specialist, Women's Studies
The Library of Congress

---

*It was agreed that Angelina and Sara Grimke, who worked closely together, would be treated as a single subject.

INTRODUCTION

In the American Revolution, the "unalienable rights" of "liberty and the pursuit of happiness" for which the colonists fought were not, in any significant way, considered to apply to women. American culture, largely imported from England, dictated a role for women — as home-maker — which allowed of few exceptions. Whatever talents beyond cooking, sewing, etc., an 18th-century American woman might have possessed, society offered little opportunity for them to be recognized, much less developed and exercised. A woman might learn to play a spinet or paint a landscape, but the study of such subjects as law or the sciences was considered dangerous to her health. Her world was the private world of the home, man's the public world of business and government. Thomas Gray's lines, "Full many a flower is born to blush unseen,/ And waste its sweetness on the desert air" touch a truth not limited in time or place, but surely, within the limits of the American experience, they tell much of the story of women in America before the 19th century.

At all times in America's history, many women found fulfillment in marriage and the home. But it was only in the 19th and 20th centuries — with a prolonged, and continuing, struggle — that women gained the opportunity to seek fulfillment in the public world of professions and careers. Only a few of the women in this book were born before 1800, and three of these (Emma Willard, Elizabeth Bayley Seton and Mary Lyon) pioneered in education, a field related to woman's traditional role as teacher in the home. But these women were also reformers, as were the Grimke sisters, Margaret Fuller, Lucy Stone and others active in the first half of the 19th century. Although the history of women's roles in American history is too complex to be addressed here, the pattern of a widening range of careers in the 19th and 20th centuries, as represented by the subjects in this book, does reflect an historical trend. The reformers of the 19th century, whether devoted primarily to suffrage or to other social causes, inevitably opened doors for those who followed — professionals like astronomer Maria Mitchell, educator Martha Carey Thomas, historian Mary Beard, and biologist Rachel Carson, as well as later reformers like physician Alice Hamilton and editor Dorothy Day. The early reformers who concentrated on the women's suffrage movement (Lucy Stone, Elizabeth Cady Stanton and Susan B. Anthony) attracted those who pursued similar careers (Frances Willard, Carrie Catt, and Alice Paul). By the end of the 19th century a few women had established themselves with remarkable success in professional careers as editors (Sarah Hale, Willa Cather) and writers (Louisa May Alcott, Harriet Beecher Stowe); by the 20th century it was possible for women to distinguish themselves in politics (Jeannette Rankin) and government (Frances Perkins, Mary McLeod Bethune), in new technologies like aviation (Amelia Earhart) and photography (Dorothea Lange, Margaret Bourke-White), and in national sports (Babe Didrikson Zaharias). None of this, it should be stressed, came without struggle.

The lives of the fifty women presented here reflect the diversity of America and yet reveal certain common traits — independence of spirit, sustained dedication to a cause or goal, and, in most cases, immense energy and courage. To be sure, they had their share of human failings — although there is one saint and others indeed saintly. But most — even one born to wealth as was Edith Wharton — did not simply accept without question the role, or the rules, that their family or American society prescribed for them. Each woman followed her own star. Each woman in her own way affected or interpreted American society and American culture. Each woman was, I believe, a human being of the dimensions Stephen Spender wrote of in his lines:

"I think continually of those who were truly great —
The names of those who in their lives fought for life,
Who wore at their hearts the fire's center.
Born of the sun they traveled a short while towards the sun,
And left the vivid air signed with their honor."

ABIGAIL ADAMS

Wife of one president (John Adams), mother of another (John Quincy Adams), Abigail Adams gained distinction not only because of the important role she played in the lives of husband and son, but also because of the remarkable life *she* led and, to an exceptional degree, recorded in over two thousand letters. Perceptive and articulate, she delineated with clarity and wit her role in — and view of — the American family, revolution, war, a new nation, foreign courts and the new capital. She is recognized as one of the great letter writers of America.

Abigail Smith had no formal education. She read widely in the library of her father, Congregationalist minister William Smith, and was helped by her brother-in-law, Richard Cranch, who introduced her to Shakespeare, Milton and Pope. She taught herself French. Some suitors were intimidated by her learning; John Adams was captivated, not least by her love letters. Their marriage was fundamentally a union of equals.

John Adams' political activities often left Abigail alone to manage their farm in Braintree, Massachusetts, and raise and educate the five children born between 1765 and 1772. She managed the farm and other business affairs so effectively, practicing "ridged oeconomy," that she gradually inherited these responsibilities, freeing her husband for public service. And she wrote letters — to John, to relatives, to friends. She knew Samuel Richardson's epistolary novels, considered him a master letter writer.

Personalities, events, ideas, impressions fill the letters that she penned almost daily. "How can women with no formal education teach their children?" she asked. She doubted Virginians' "passion for Liberty" since they "have been accustomed to deprive their fellow Creatures of theirs." To John in Congress contemplating independence, she wrote: "Remember the Ladies, and be more generous and favourable to them than your ancestors.... If particular care...is not paid to the Ladies we are determined to foment a Rebellion, and will not hold ourselves bound by any Laws in which we have no voice, or Representation."

Throughout John Adams' career, the well-informed Abigail served as his advisor and alter ego; her letters to him in Europe offered news, advice, encouragement. In England with him — as first American Minister — she endured royal disdain, but she also noted the tyranny of the aristocracy, from which John Adams had helped free Americans. Her letters contain refreshingly candid observations on court society in France and England: she was appalled by the lavish display, the pomp and pageantry.

When her husband became president, Abigail was accused of having too much influence over the President — certainly she was more involved than Martha Washington had been. She was the first First Lady to move into the new President's House on the Potomac, a "great castle" which, she observed, "is built for ages to come."

Abigail's interest in John Quincy's career never diminished; he, too, received letters — and advice. He served with distinction in diplomatic posts in Europe and was secretary of state when Abigail died, six years before he was elected president.

1744   Born Nov. 11 Weymouth, Mass.

1764   Married John Adams

1784-85   Lived in France

1785-88   Lived in England

1797-1801   John Adams, President of the United States

1818   Died Oct. 28, Quincy, Mass.

JANE ADDAMS

The founder of Hull House and the settlement in America, Jane Addams championed broad social reforms in the United States and, during and after World War I, was a leader of the international women's peace movement — for which she was awarded the Nobel Prize.

Influenced by her father, an abolitionist and friend of Lincoln's, and by zealous teachers at Rockford Seminary, young Jane determined "that I should study medicine and live with the poor." She did not take to medical study, but in a London settlement she visited in 1888 she saw the vehicle for serving America's poor. The next year she moved into the old Hull mansion in Chicago's tenement section; Hull House quickly became the center of the neglected, largely immigrant community, providing a nursery and dispensary, as well as job-training, education and recreation — everything from sewing courses to concerts: social justice and the arts under one roof. It became the model for the American settlement house, the place where over-privileged, idealistic young women could serve and "live with the poor."

Hull House became a force beyond neighborhood services; Addams supported legislation on child labor, industrial safety, sweatshops, etc. Her articles and lectures carried her views on social justice beyond Illinois. Her books — *City Streets*, a study of immigrant families, and *Twenty Years in Hull House* — were widely read. By 1910 there were hundreds of "Hull Houses."

The success of Hull House brought Jane Addams recognition — an honorary degree from Yale — and added responsibilities. She was elected to office in national social service organizations. She became politically active, shocking some when, in 1912, she campaigned for Theodore Roosevelt and his Progressive Party, which was pledged to many of the reforms that Hull House had long sought. She actively supported the suffrage movement and held office in the national association. Several times she was called upon to settle labor disputes.

Although most of the work of Hull House won praise at home and abroad, Jane Addams' campaigns for labor reform and the open discussions she fostered at Hull House, often concentrating on social issues, led some wealthy patrons to brand her a radical — and withdraw support — but Hull House weathered such storms.

Jane Addams endured far worse for her uncompromising stand against war. An outspoken pacifist (author of *Newer Ideals of Peace*, 1907), she emerged, after war began, as a leader of an international peace movement. When she persisted in her stand after the U.S. declared war, she was vilified by newspapers and politicians — and expelled from the Daughters of the American Revolution. But she refused to compromise: to this champion of social justice, war was the supreme social evil.

For years after the war Jane Addams presided over the Women's International League for Peace and Freedom, and in 1928, over a Pan-Pacific conference in Hawaii. The mild-mannered, persistent pacifist became at last a beloved world figure — the first American woman awarded the Nobel Prize.

BY GEORGE DEFOREST BRUSH

1860　Born Sep. 6 Cedarville, Ill.

1881　Graduated from Rockford Female Seminary

1881-82　Attended Women's Medical College of Pennsylvania

1889　Founded Hull House

1909　Published *The Spirit of Youth and the City Streets*

1910　Published *Twenty Years at Hull House*

1911-14　Vice-President, National American Woman's Suffrage Assoc.

1911-35　President, National Federation of Settlements

1915　Chairman, Woman's Peace Party

1915　President, International Congress of Women

1919-35　President, Women's International League for Peace and Freedom

1920　Helped found American Civil Liberties Union

1931　Awarded the Nobel Peace Prize

1935　Died May 21 Chicago, Ill.

LOUISA MAY ALCOTT

Little Women, Louisa May Alcott's story of Meg, Jo, Beth and Amy March, is an American classic, a 19th-century novel which, according to Alcott's biographer, "defines the dream of American family life." One of the first best-selling novels (38,000 copies in 1869), the book established Miss Alcott as the premiere popular author of the American domestic scene, and she responded by producing over twenty more novels and collections of stories.

Like Jo March, Louisa was the second of four daughters — and all play idealized roles in *Little Women*. Her father, Bronson Alcott, was a totally impractical idealist, schoolmaster and educational innovator. A stern moralist who prescribed *Pilgrim's Progress* and the meatless diet of Sylvester Graham (of cracker fame), he provided more precepts than support; his wife, Abigail, was the anchor of the family, much closer to Louisa than the abstracted father.

After Bronson Alcott's Temple School in Boston failed in 1840, the family moved to Concord, where Louisa attended the school of Henry and John Thoreau; there she wrote her first poem — and met Emerson and Hawthorne. The family moved often, once almost starving at Fruitlands, a utopian community Bronson Alcott organized near Harvard, Massachusetts. The father's repeated failures deeply affected Louisa; in her journal she resolved — at 13 — to "teach, sew, act, write, anything to help the family." For fun she wrote plays which she and her sisters staged in their kitchen.

Miss Alcott's first published story appeared in the *Saturday Evening Gazette* in 1854, under the name "Flora Fairfield," followed by a collection of fairy stories, under her own name. She moved, alone, to Boston and worked as a seamstress, teacher and domestic to supplement her earnings from writing thrillers and lurid tales under various pseudonyms, sending home what she could. Her service as an Army nurse in Washington during the Civil War, cut short by a near-fatal illness, provided experiences that became "Hospital Sketches," which appeared in serial and book form, and won favorable notice. After she wrote a romance — *Moods* — that was moderately successful, a publisher and the family urged her to try a domestic novel about young girls.

She moved from Boston to the family house in Concord — the scene of much of the novel — to write the first volume, which was published in September 1868; on January 1, 1869, she finished the second volume. The characters were, essentially, her own family, the theme that of *Pilgrim's Progress*. Each of the Alcott daughters is readily recognizable: in the character of long-suffering Jo, Louisa poured much of herself. The transmuted Abba Alcott is the saintly Marmee, who dominates the home; her prominent role — with the fictional father absent — provided a model for later generations of American women.

The novel reached a new, middle-class readership; its success brought Miss Alcott the security she had long sought for her family, but she forged on, writing sketches and stories as well as sequels to *Little Women*, which remains — with millions sold — still popular today.

1832	Born Nov. 29 Germantown, Penn.	1870	Published *An Old-Fashioned Girl*
1854	Published *Flower Fables*	1871	Published *Little Men*
1862-63	Nurse, U.S. Army	1875	Published *Eight Cousins*
1863	Published *Hospital Sketches*	1880	Published *Jack & Jill*
1864	Published *Moods*	1886	Published *Jo's Boys*
1868-69	Published *Little Women*	1888	Died Mar. 6 Boston, Mass.

SUSAN B. ANTHONY

"The Napoleon of the women's rights movement," William Channing called her, and no pioneer of that movement in America was more totally dedicated to the cause. From her father, who opposed slavery, and from the Quaker meeting, which taught equality before God, Susan Anthony gained a strong sense of independence and moral zeal, and, once drawn to the women's movement, she made it *her* cause and devoted herself to it unstintingly for over half a century.

After teaching for ten years, Susan Anthony returned home to help manage the family farm. There she met abolitionist Lloyd Garrison, Amelia Bloomer and Elizabeth Cady Stanton, and became active in temperance work. When she was not permitted to speak at a temperance rally, she and Cady Stanton promptly formed a *women's* temperance society, the first of its kind, and an alliance that would keep them at the forefront of the women's movement for decades.

Miss Anthony, who remained single, had the freedom to perform a role — as a traveling organizer — that suited her talents. Lacking the personality and speaking ability of Stanton, she was most effective working behind the scenes. For years she toured the East winning support, obtaining signatures on petitions, and giving lectures, even though she recognized her shortcomings as a speaker. She frequently encountered abuse, sometimes violence.

Anthony and Stanton's campaigns in New York in the 1850s led to improved laws concerning property rights for women. During the Civil War they obtained hundreds of thousands of signatures supporting emancipation legislation, but their alliance with abolitionists brought little support for women's suffrage. They saw the 14th Amendment, giving *male* Negroes the vote, as betrayal of their cause. For two years they published a weekly, *Revolution*, which crusaded for the cause of women; its motto: "Men Their Rights and Nothing More — Women Their Rights and Nothing Less." In 1869 they founded the National Woman Suffrage Association, the first national organization devoted primarily to women's suffrage. Its principal goal was a Federal women's suffrage amendment. Later that year the American Woman Suffrage Association was formed by Lucy Stone and others who favored action through the States.

Susan Anthony was arrested for voting illegally in the 1872 Presidential election; she refused to pay the fine. Later she and Cady Stanton persuaded Senator Aaron Sargent of California to introduce a women's suffrage amendment in the U.S. Senate. With Stanton and Matilda Gage, Anthony wrote the comprehensive *History of Woman Suffrage*. Differences between the two suffrage groups were resolved in 1890; they formed the National American Woman Suffrage Association, dedicated to both a Federal amendment and State approval.

By 1900 Susan Anthony had gained a measure of acceptance for her cause and recognition as its foremost leader. At eighty, she retired from the presidency of the national association. Six years later, at the last suffrage convention she would attend, she delivered her final declaration: "Failure is impossible."

1820   Born Feb. 15 Adams, Mass.

1837-38   Attended Friends Seminary, Philadelphia, Penn.

1839-45   Teacher, Friends Seminary, New Rochelle, N.Y.

1846-49   Head, Female Dept., Canajoharie Academy, Rochester, N.Y.

1852   Founded N.Y. State Women's Temperance Society

1868   Formed Working Women's Association (With Mrs. Stanton)

1868-69   Publisher, *Revolution* (Weekly newspaper)

1869   Founded National Woman Suffrage Association (With Mrs. Stanton)

1881   Published first volume of *History of Woman Suffrage*

1892-1900   President, National American Woman Suffrage Association

1906   Died Mar. 13 Rochester, N.Y.

17

ETHEL BARRYMORE

Ethel Barrymore was born to the stage — and spent much of her life there. Her father was matinee-idol Maurice Barrymore, her mother comedienne Georgiana Drew, with eight generations in the theater before *her*. For half a century Ethel starred in theatrical performances in America and England, playing an astonishing variety of roles; with her vibrant voice and commanding presence, she won international acclaim on the stage and in films, receiving an Academy Award for her performance with Cary Grant in *None But the Lonely Heart*.

As a child, Ethel play-acted with her brothers — John and Lionel — in an old barn. At 15, she was playing small parts in the theater. A three-year apprenticeship with her uncle John Drew's company prepared her for her first leading role, in *His Excellency the Governor* (1900), and her first starring role, in *Captain Jinks . . .* (1901). She made her first of many London appearances in 1897.

The next decade found her an established star, featured in *A Country Mouse* (1903), *Sunday* (1904) — in which she improvised the line, "That's all there is, there isn't any more," Ibsen's *The Doll House* (1905), and Maugham's *Lady Frederick* (1908). By 1910 she had become a romantic idol, worshipped by men, imitated by women (her clothes, voice, walk).

After she married Russell Colt, son of the president of U.S. Rubber Co., she continued to perform. They had three children. The marriage ended in divorce, and Barrymore, a Catholic, never remarried.

From 1914 to 1918 she made thirteen films, but at that time she preferred the stage, where she starred in such successes as *Tante* (1913), *Our Mrs. McChesney* (1915), *The Lady of the Camellias* (1917) and *Declasseé* (1919), in which she broke attendance records at the Empire Theatre.

When Actors Equity went on strike in 1919, Barrymore stood with "her people": "All we are working for," she wrote, "is democracy in the theatre, justice, equality, truth." She performed in benefits and represented the union in signing the hard-won agreement.

Ethel Barrymore had her critical failures — as Juliet in *Romeo and Juliet* (1922) and Lady Teazle in *School for Scandal* (1923), but her performances in other Shakespearean roles (Ophelia, Portia), played with Walter Hampden, and in *The Second Mrs. Tanqueray* (1924) and *The Constant Wife* (1924), brought high praise.

The Ethel Barrymore Theatre in New York opened in 1928 with Ethel as Sister Garcia (aging from 19 to 70) in *The Kingdom of God*. In *Scarlet Sister Mary* (1930) she played a black. One of her most memorable roles was as Miss Moffat in *The Corn is Green* (1940).

Ethel's only appearance with brothers John and Lionel was in the film *Rasputin and the Empress* (1932). After she made *None But the Lonely Heart* she settled in California and made twenty more films as well as television shows.

Ethel Barrymore was one of America's most versatile, most accomplished actresses: the beautiful young heroine of comedy and drama matured to character parts, moving surely from stage to silent to sound films to television.

BY JAMES MONTGOMERY FLAGG

1879   Born Aug. 16 Philadelphia, Penn.

1894   Stage debut in *The Rivals*

1897   London debut in *Secret Service*

1898- Member, Stock Company, Empire Theater

1901   First starring role in *Captain Jinks of the Horse Marines*

1909   Married Russell Colt; divorced 1923

1914   Appeared in first film, *The Nightingale*

1944   Academy Award — Best Actress, *None But The Lonely Heart*

1946   Speech Medal, American Academy of Arts & Letters

1959   Died Jun. 18 Beverly Hills, Calif.

CLARA BARTON

In the Civil War, Clara Barton fought on the side of humanity, and she continued to fight human suffering as founder and first president of the American Red Cross.

As a child Clara nursed her brother David for two years. At 15, she began teaching. Serving others proved deeply satisfying to this shy, determined girl. In New Jersey she started a free school; when it succeeded, a man was appointed over her. She promptly resigned.

Miss Barton was working at the Patent Office in Washington when the Civil War began. Amidst the tumult, she saw the need for provisions and medical supplies; on her own she advertised for contributions. She stored bandages, medicine and food in her rooms and, with Army mule teams, personally distributed them to the lines. On battlefields she tended the wounded and dying. "I wrung the blood from the bottom of my clothing before I could step," she wrote. Resourceful and independent, she ignored red tape, bringing food and aid to thousands. A surgeon wrote: ". . . if heaven ever sent out a holy angel, she must be one."

After the war she established an information center serving families and missing soldiers, and aided in identifying and marking thousands of graves. She lectured extensively. In 1868, exhausted, she suffered a breakdown and went to Switzerland.

While recuperating, Miss Barton learned of the international Red Cross, established in Switzerland in 1864. Its Geneva Treaty, which guaranteed the neutrality of hospitals in future wars, was ratified by eleven nations, but the U.S. was against ratification, primarily because the Monroe Doctrine prohibited international treaties. After Miss Barton returned, she began a solitary crusade to establish the Red Cross in America. She took her cause to Washington and, through articles and speeches, to the American public. She emphasized the proposed peacetime role of the Red Cross in providing relief to victims of droughts, floods and other non-military disasters. She organized the American Association of the Red Cross in 1881. The next year the United States ratified the Geneva Treaty.

As president of the Red Cross, Clara Barton directed operations with a firm hand. The new organization provided relief to victims of a Michigan forest fire, an East Coast hurricane — even a Russian famine. Fearing official control, Miss Barton refused government funds: all money came directly from private citizens. Her small group promptly supplied food, clothing and medicine where needed; soon it added tools and materials for rehabilitation.

During the Spanish-American War, Clara Barton, now seventy-seven, was again on a mule wagon distributing provisions. But her intense personal involvement and informal methods, which originally helped in building and maintaining a small effective group, became less and less appropriate to a growing national organization.

The five-foot tall woman with the large heart proved to be a better founder than manager; she stayed too long and, with some bitterness, reluctantly resigned from her post. But she has accomplished her mission: "Everybody's business is nobody's business," she had said, ". . . nobody's business is my business."

1821   Born Dec. 25 North Oxford, Mass.

1836-54   Teacher, Elementary Schools, Mass. & N.J.

1850   Attended Liberal Institute, Clinton, N.Y.

1854-57 ⎰ Clerk, U.S. Patent Office,
1860-61 ⎱ Washington, D.C.

1861-65   Volunteer Nurse, U.S. Army

1881   Organized American Red Cross

1881-1904   President, American Red Cross

1906   Organized National First Aid Association of America

1912   Died Apr. 12 Washington, D.C.

MARY BEARD

Historian Mary Beard championed women in a way unique for her time — and ours: in the long history of civilization, she observed, women played a dominant role in society by assuming primary responsibility for the "continuance and care of life," by creating and sustaining the domestic arts, by nurturing and transmitting culture, and ultimately, by her influence in the public sphere through these private roles. Although she co-authored a distinguished series on American history, she concentrated her efforts on the neglected history of women, creating the intellectual foundation for the formal study of women's history.

Mary Ritter met Charles Beard at DePauw University. They spent their first married years in England, Charles studying, Mary involving herself in woman-suffrage and trade-union movements. When Charles began teaching at Columbia University, Mary continued as a social activist: she joined the National Women's Trade Union League and the Woman Suffrage Party. She served as editor of the party's *The Woman Voter*. In 1913 she became a member of Alice Paul's Congressional Committee, the most radical element of the National American Woman Suffrage Association. Mary Beard wrote articles, spoke, and testified before Congressional hearings; she remained with Paul when the latter broke with the national organization and formed the Congressional Union (later the Woman's Party).

Beard's concern for the plight of workingwomen led her to write *Woman's Work in Municipalities*, a penetrating analysis of the social roles of women, and eventually to split with Paul over the Equal Rights Amendment. Beard and other feminists like physician Alice Hamilton believed that women in certain kinds of work required special conditions and treatment and, in fact, had secured legislation to protect them; to Beard, the ERA would jeopardize all that they had accomplished.

Gradually Mary Beard shifted from political activist to analyst and critic — with her own distinctive view of women. In *On Understanding Women* she developed the thesis that woman is "the elemental force in the rise and development of Civilization." "When kings, priests, and noble classes . . . engaged the attention of historians," she wrote, "women merely dropped out of the pen portraits. They remained in actuality." She cited Sappho, Jeanne d'Arc, Heloise, Queen Isabella as a few history remembered. The idea that women had been an oppressed group was, she believed, false to history, a myth that gave women a distorted image of their past.

In the history series she co-authored, Beard wove details of women's contributions into the sweeping survey. The Beards created one of the most balanced — and the most successful — works on American history in the Twentieth Century. To overcome ignorance about women in history, Beard tried to establish a permanent archives, the World Center for Women's Archives; after five years the effort failed, but libraries in several women's colleges now perform that function. In *Woman as Force in History* Beard analyzed English law to demonstrate that American feminists misunderstood the history of legal language when they adopted the theory of women's total subjugation at the Seneca Falls Convention in 1848.

1876 Born Aug. 5 Indianapolis, Ind.

1897 Graduated from DePauw University

1900 Married Charles Beard

1902-04 Attended Columbia University

1915 Published *Women's Work in Municipalities*

1920 Published *A Short History of the American Labor Movement*

1927 Published *The Rise of American Civilization* (With Charles Beard), Vols. 1 & 2

1931 Published *On Understanding Women*

1933 Published *America Through Women's Eyes*

1939 Published *The Rise of American Civilization,* Vols. 3 & 4

1942 Published *The Rise of American Civilization,* Vol. 5

1946 Published *Woman as Force in History*

1958 Died Aug. 14 Phoenix, Ariz.

MARY McLEOD BETHUNE

Born in a log cabin, the fifteenth child of freed slaves, Mary McLeod Bethune became a college president, an advisor to presidents, and spokeswoman for her race. A charismatic figure, a blend of charm and steel, she unflinchingly fought for opportunities for blacks in education and American society generally. As advisor to President Franklin Roosevelt, she was one of the most powerful and respected blacks in America.

A precocious child, Mary McLeod won a scholarship to Scotia Seminary, where she took teacher training (a true soprano, she also studied voice), and another to Moody Bible Institute in Chicago, where she studied to be a missionary. Deeply religious, she sought assignment in Africa, but there were no openings and she turned to teaching — with a missionary's zeal. While teaching in Sumter, S.C., she met Albertus Bethune; they were married and had one child. After Mary started a mission school in Palatka, Florida, they separated.

Mary Bethune's dream was to establish a school for black girls; when she learned Daytona, Florida, was in need of one, she moved there. With "$1.50 and faith" — and boxes and packing cases for chairs and desks, she started her school. Five girls were in the first class. Mary Bethune taught; she went door to door for donations and persuaded prominent industrialists to serve as trustees. In the face of poverty and prejudice, the school grew: land, a building — Faith Hall, a campus. Daytona Literary and Industrial Institute, offering basic courses and social programs for adults, as well as religious and industrial education for girls, became a positive force in the community.

A superb administrator, Mary Bethune established a hospital for blacks, added a normal school to the Institute and, in 1923, founded — and became president of — Bethune-Cookman Collegiate Institute, bringing the school for black males under her direction.

Mary Bethune's strong, trained voice and dynamic personality equipped her well for the role of college spokeswoman; as the college grew, the scope of her travel — and influence — increased. She addressed groups large and small, ranging to major Northern cities. After serving as president of the Florida Federation of Colored Women, she became president of the National Association of Colored Women, a national pulpit she used to speak out for racial equality, presenting herself as one who felt obliged to use her opportunities to ease the way for others. She established the NACW's first permanent headquarters in Washington.

Mary Bethune served on presidential commissions under Presidents Coolidge and Hoover; President Roosevelt selected her to head the Division of Negro Affairs in the National Youth Administration and to serve as advisor on minority affairs. She organized the Federal Council on Negro Affairs, a group of black leaders in govenment who worked to help blacks participate in government and utilize its services.

Mary Bethune succeeded in reducing barriers and opening doors for blacks in America, providing also an example of individual achievement which embodies the best of America.

1875 Born Jul. 10 Mayesville, S.C.

1894 Graduated from Scotia Seminary, Concord, N.C.

1904 Founded Daytona Normal & Industrial Institute, Daytona, Fla.

1923 Daytona Institute merged with Cookman Institute

1924-28 President, National Association of Colored Women

1935 Founded National Council of Negro Women

1935 Member, Advisory Committee, U.S. National Youth Administration

1936-44 Director, Division of Negro Affairs, National Youth Administration

1940-55 Vice-President, National Association for the Advancement of Colored People

1943 Bethune-Cookman conferred first college degrees

1945 Consultant, United Nations Conference

1955 Died May 18 Daytona Beach, Fla.

MARGARET BOURKE-WHITE

She was one of the first photojournalists — and perhaps photohistorians — in America: she witnessed and recorded, with artistry and telling accuracy, an amazing number of the great triumphs and catastrophes of the second quarter of the 20th century. A fearless and untiring adventurer, Margaret Bourke-White took her camera anywhere — from the top of a New York skyscraper to the death camps of Buchenwald — to capture in memorable photographs what man had accomplished, what man had done to man.

Margaret took a course in photography in college but majored in biology; it was merely an avocation until her senior year when, after a failed marriage, she sold photographs to pay expenses. Photographs of campus buildings led her briefly into architectural photography, but she became fascinated with modern technology: her pictures of the works of a Cleveland steel mill depict a dynamism and drama then unique in industrial photographs. Confronted with extremes of heat and light, she mastered the technical limits of camera, film and paper.

A job with the new magazine *Fortune* provided Bourke-White a wide range of subjects — making glass, mining bauxite, building skyscrapers — and new challenges. A group of photographs of the butchering of hogs had a narrative sequence that foreshadowed the later photographic essay. She had been captivated by the esthetic of the machine, but she went beyond it. In the Thirties, trips to Germany yielded dramatic industrial images but also ominous pictures of military training and maneuvers; trips to Russia brought stark, eloquent photographs of man and machines — some firsts from the Soviet Union. Coverage of the American Dust Bowl and the ravages of the drought presaged her collaborative photo-documentary (with Erskine Caldwell) on the sharecroppers in the South, with its devastating pictures of human decay — her most socially significant work. She and Caldwell married — and produced other documentaries: a study of pre-war Czechoslovakia and a sweeping survey of the U.S.

Life magazine — designed to feature photographs — further extended Bourke-White's horizons. She did *Life's* first cover story (on a dam in the West), its first photo essay, and 283 other assignments over a twenty-year period: portraits of Churchill and Stalin, Moscow being bombed by German planes, and U.S. forces in action in World War II. She flew on a U.S. bombing mission, covered General Patton's advance into Germany, and photographed the "living dead" of Buchenwald. She took portraits of the defeated Herman Goring and the jubilant Soviet Marshall Zhukov, aerial views of war-ravaged German cities.

After the war she covered the birth of the nations of Pakistan and India and took one of the last portraits of Gandhi. In South Africa she went a mile underground to photograph gold miners known only by numbers; in South Korea she recorded the human cost of the war.

Thousands of photographs testify to Bourke-White's talents: the instinct of the journalist, the sure eye of the artist, and an unfailing resolve to render facts honestly.

1904 Born Jun. 14 New York, N.Y.

1922-23 Attended Columbia University

1923-25 Attended University of Michigan

1926 Married Everett Chapman; divorced 1927

1926-27 Attended Cornell University

1929- Photographer, *Fortune* magazine

1931 Published *Eyes on Russia*

1936- Photographer, *Life* magazine

1937 Published *You Have Seen Their Faces* (With Erskine Caldwell)

1939 Married Erskine Caldwell; divorced 1942

1939 Published *North of the Danube* (With E. Caldwell)

1941 Published *Say, Is This the U.S.A.?* (With E. Caldwell)

1971 Died Aug. 27 Stanford, Conn.

SOPHONISBA BRECKENRIDGE

Scholar, teacher, reformer, social activist — Sophonisba Breckenridge influenced — and participated in — a remarkable number of the major reform movements in America during the first decades of the 20th century. A dynamo in the classroom and in her struggles for reform, she was an agent for social change out of all proportion to her size (90 lbs.).

The daughter of lawyer, Congressman and Confederate Colonel William Breckenridge, Sophonisba, after graduating from Wellesley, studied in her father's law office and was the first woman to pass the bar examination in Kentucky. At the University of Chicago she earned a PhD in political science (first woman to do so) and a JD, and then began a teaching career that spanned almost forty years.

In 1907 Miss Breckenridge launched her career as an activist: she joined the Women's Trade Union League, became a resident of Jane Addam's Hull House, and began teaching at both the University and the Chicago School of Civics and Philanthropy, where she trained social workers. After she became head of the school's research department (1908), Sophonisba and her assistant, Edith Abbot, started collecting information first-hand by observing life in Chicago's teeming West Side, from which they produced studies of family life under such conditions.

The city became more than Miss Breckenridge's laboratory; she was drawn into welfare administration and reform movements. She inspected tenements for the city health department, fought for child labor laws, evaluated Chicago's juvenile court system, helped establish the Immigrants' Protective League and the National Association for the Advancement of Colored People, and served the suffragist cause as vice president of the National American Woman's Suffrage Association. She assisted women's trade unions, drafting legal bills to regulate the conditions of women's employment. As an officer of the Women's City Club of Chicago and the American Association of University Women, she helped direct the women's club movement into the work of social reform. With Jane Addams she helped form the Woman's Peace Party (1915).

Through these years Miss Breckenridge continued to teach — for the department of household administration at the University and for the School of Civics and Philanthropy. She was primarily responsible for bringing the School, never too successful, into the University as the Graduate School of Social Service Administration. As professor of social economy and, after 1929, Samuel Deutsch Professor of Public Welfare Administration, she influenced the development of a unique professional program for social workers combining extensive academic study with welfare work. In her courses and publications she advocated the direct involvement of the state in social welfare programs; graduates of her courses established some of the first public welfare programs developed to meet the needs of the Great Depression.

Generations of students attested to the power of Miss Breckenridge's blend of knowledge, conviction and charm. Through her books and the professional journal she founded and edited, *Social Service Review,* she influenced many more. In addition to professional recognition, President Roosevelt appointed her delegate to the Pan-American Congress in Montevideo in 1933, the first woman so honored.

1866	Born Apr. 1 Lexington, Ky.
1888	Graduated from Wellesley College
1901	Received PhD from University of Chicago
1902-	Assistant Dean of Women, University of Chicago
1904	Received JD from University of Chicago
1904-42	Instructor, professor, University of Chicago
1907-	Instructor, Chicago School of Civics & Philanthropy

1912	Published *The Modern Household* (With Marion Talbot)
1912	Published *The Delinquent Child and the Home* (With Edith Abbott)
1915	Delegate, International Congress of Women, The Hague
1921	Published *New Homes for Old* (With Edith Abbott)
1927	Published *Public Welfare Administration*
1934	Published *The Family and the State*
1948	Died Jul. 30 Chicago, Ill.

29

RACHEL CARSON

"I can remember no time when I wasn't interested in the out-of-doors and the whole world of nature," Rachel Carson wrote, and two of her books — *The Sea Around Us* and *Silent Spring* — dramatically changed the way man comprehends the sea and values and preserves "the whole world of nature." Her scientific analysis of the pervasive effect of the use of pesticides alerted the world to the mounting danger to all living things: publication of *Silent Spring* marked the beginning of the modern environmental movement.

Rachel Carson grew up in the country. Her mother, a former teacher, encouraged her interest in books and in nature, and Rachel aspired to be a writer. In college she majored in English; after a course in biology she switched to zoology.

Carson first began to study the sea at the Marine Biological Laboratory at Woods Hole, Massachusetts. She was one of the first women hired as an aquatic biologist by the U.S. Bureau of Fisheries. Articles she wrote about fisheries were published by the Baltimore *Sun*. Her first major article on the sea, "Undersea," published in *The Atlantic Monthly*, attracted the attention of book-editor Quincy Howe and author Hendrik van Loon; both encouraged her to do a book. *Under the Sea Wind,* published weeks before Pearl Harbor, sold few copies but was praised by reviewers and scientists.

Rachel Carson's writings for the government revealed the same crisp precision and style that distinguished her first book: she wrote bulletins on seafood for consumers during the war, and later a series of booklets on wildlife refuges rich with detail masterfully rendered. And she performed extensive research for a second, more comprehensive, book on the sea.

The Sea Around Us took the world — and Rachel Carson — by surprise. Advance publication in *The New Yorker* brought an unprecedented response from readers. The book, published July 2, 1951, was almost immediately sold out. Reviewers raved about it; it stayed on the best-seller list for eighty-six weeks, was eventually published in thirty-two languages. In accepting the National Book Award, Carson modestly observed: "The winds, the sea and the moving tides are what they are. If there is wonder and beauty and majesty in them, science will discover these qualities . . . ," but it took a scientist with the pen of a poet to capture both the "facts" and the beauty and majesty, to create a classic.

The increasing use of DDT and other nonselective poisons led Carson to write *Silent Spring*. She described how such poisons accumulate in plants and animals; how they reach rivers and lakes, endangering the fish, and then the birds — and humans — who eat the fish; how they dangerously threaten the balance of nature and all life. The book created a tumult of controversy: the chemical industry attacked Carson, but scientists and the President's Science Advisory Committee supported her findings. *Silent Spring* proved to be one of the most influential books of its time.

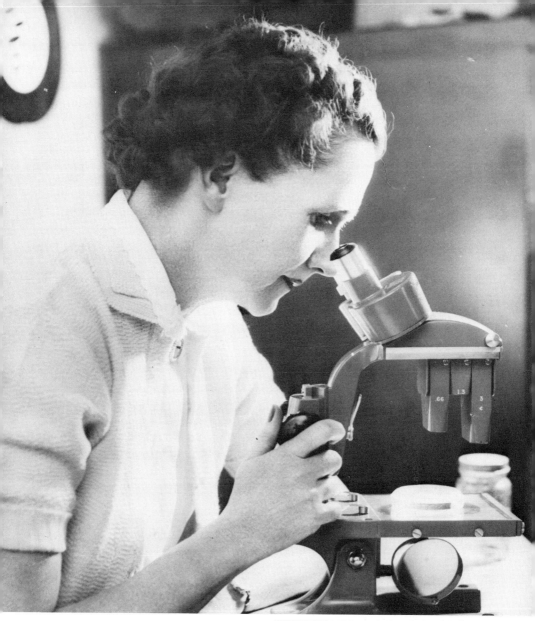

1907	Born May 27 Springdale, Penn.
1929	Graduated fron Pennsylvania College for Women
1932	Received MA, Johns Hopkins University
1928-	(Summers) Student, Marine Biological Laboratory, Woods Hole, Mass.
1928-35	Teacher, University of Maryland, Johns Hopkins U.
1935-49	Biologist, U.S. Bureau of Fisheries
1941	Published *Under the Sea-Wind*
1949-52	Chief Editor, U.S. Fish & Wildlife Service
1951	Published *The Sea Around Us*
1955	Published *The Edge of the Sea*
1962	Published *Silent Spring*
1963	Member, American Academy of Arts & Letters
1964	Died Apr. 14 Silver Spring, Md.

MARY CASSATT

"I will not admit that a woman can draw like that," Edgar Degas said on seeing a picture of Mary Cassatt's. Other Impressionist painters — Camille Pissarro and Paul Gaugin — also admired her work; she joined their group — in Paris in the 1870s — and under their influence developed a style that incorporated certain elements of Impressionism yet was distinctively her own. Her Impressionist paintings were the first exhibited in America.

At 16, Mary Cassatt was determined to be a painter — in spite of her father's objections. At the Pennsylvania Academy, the formal academic instruction proved limiting and frustrating, and as independent as she was determined, she went to Europe to study on her own. Only after extended study of Correggio's works in Parma (1872) and Rubens' in Antwerp (1873) did she begin to progress beyond rigid academic renditions.

At the Paris Salon of 1874 Degas first saw — and admired — a Cassatt painting: "Madame Cortier", a portrait of simplicity, boldness and masterful control. Painstakingly thorough — and slow — in her development, Miss Cassatt had, at 30, earned the praise of the most uncompromising of the Impressionists. As one of their group, she worked with Degas, and his influence is evident in her later pieces (In a letter Mary Cassatt acknowledged that Degas "even worked on" the background of *"Le Salon Bleu".)*.

Both Mary Cassatt and Degas came from aristocratic families, with similar tastes and sensibilities: besides her artistic talent, Degas admired her frankness and decisiveness. Others saw her differently. The American artist George Biddle observed: "She was one of the most vital, high-minded, dedicated and prejudiced human beings I have ever known . . . ."

Cassatt paintings in the Impressionist exhibitions received favorable reviews from Paris critics: by 1879 she had won a place of distinction in the Paris art world, yet she was scarcely known in America.

Cassatt's parents and sister joined her in Paris in 1877. They lived comfortably in Paris and in the country, family life only a minor distraction to the dedicated painter. Members of the family often served as models.

A sensitive collector herself, Mary Cassatt assisted in selecting paintings for two American collections — her brother Alexander's and Mrs. Louisine Havemeyer's — and was thus instrumental in introducing Degas and other Impressionists to America in the 1870s. Most of the Havemeyer Collection is now in the Metropolitan Museum.

Cassatt's work was not confined to oils. She shared Degas' interest in pastels and produced sensitive pastels of Mrs. Havemeyer and daughter, and other figures. An exhibition of Japanese prints at *Beaux Arts* in 1890 strongly influenced her graphic work, particularly a series of ten aquatints, considered some of her finest creations. As a disciplined draftsman, she welcomed the challenge of printmaking, where there is no room for error.

For the Woman's Building of the Columbian Exposition of 1893, Mary Cassatt painted an undistinguished mural depicting Modern Woman. Her best works were portraits and small groupings. She repeatedly portrayed a mother and child, with variations of scene, scale and mood, always avoiding sentimentality. She was America's foremost woman painter.

SELF PORTRAIT   **THE METROPOLITAN MUSEUM OF ART**

1844 Born May 22 Allegheny City, Penn.

1865 Graduated from Pennsylvania Academy of the Fine Arts

1872 First painting exhibited (at Paris salon)

1876 First painting exhibited in America

1879 First painting shown at Impressionist Exhibit

1893 Painted mural for Columbian Exposition

1926 Died Jun. 14 Mesnil-Theribus, France

WILLA CATHER

One of America's foremost novelists of the frontier, Willa Cather memorably depicted the prairie and the human qualities of the men and women of the frontier — the great vitality, imagination and heroism — in a series of compelling works. With what Oliver Wendell Holmes called the "gift of the transfiguring touch," she wrote stories which celebrate and compassionately render the texture of frontier life.

After spending her first ten years on a farm in Virginia, Willa Cather was abruptly uprooted when the family moved to Nebraska — a wrenching experience that made her spiritual kin of the Swedes, Bohemians and Russians she found living in wind-swept sod houses on the open prairie.

Although her talent was evident in the oration she delivered at her high school commencement, Miss Cather matured slowly as a writer. She spent over sixteen years working as a reporter, reviewer and editor for newspapers and magazines before completing her first novel, *Alexander's Masquerade*. Novelist Sarah Orne Jewett helped her achieve her own style and influenced her to abandon journalism and concentrate on fiction.

After she left her editorial post at *McClure's*, Willa Cather devoted herself to writing. *O Pioneers!* the first of the prairie novels, pursues the theme dominating most of the novels: the struggle of a strong-willed person for success and — in some works — the realization of the hollowness of success. The central figures in *O Pioneers!* and *My Antonia* — Alexandra and Antonia — are exceptions in that they succeed in creating satisfying lives without the ensuing bitterness; they represent the early — heroic — pioneer stock that Cather tended to romanticize. *One of Ours*, which won the Pulitzer Prize, and *A Lost Lady* depict what Cather saw as the end of an era on the prairie — the decline of the pioneer tradition and the loss of a kind of greatness. With the advent of the machine, life became stultifying, dull. To Cather, the machine was a villain, an agent of change that violated the rich land and smothered the human spirit.

For her most popular — and best — later novels, Cather turned to the figures of pioneers in history — in the early American Southwest and in French Canada. *Death Comes for the Archbishop* and *Shadows on the Rock* present powerful leaders — a French prelate and a French count — struggling to bring Catholicism and French culture to new lands.

It is significant that Cather, after she exhausted her Nebraska experience, went further into the past for new material. She did not take to the 20th century; she resisted change, and her best work consisted of recollected experience — the early pioneers who endured and prevailed and the vast prairie that had both tormented and enchanted her.

A superb stylist, Willa Cather etched the conquest of the frontier in tales remarkable, particularly, for the poetic painting of the land and nature. Her descriptions of landscapes and weather have been compared to those of Turgenev. She caught the spell and wonder of the endless prairie and probed the human victories over the vanishing frontier.

1873 Born Dec. 7 Back Creek Valley, Va.

1883 Moved to Webster City, Neb.

1895 Graduated from University of Nebraska

1895-96 Newspaper Reporter, Lincoln, Neb.

1896-97 Editor, *Home Monthly* magazine

1897-1906 Editor, reviewer, *Pittsburg Daily Leader*

1903 Published *April Twilights* (verse)

1905 Published *The Troll Garden* (short stories)

1906-12 Editor, *McClure's* magazine

1912 *Alexander's Masquerade* (novel) serialized in *McClure's*

1913 Published *O Pioneers!*

1915 Published *Song of the Lark*

1918 Published *My Antonia*

1921 Published *One of Ours*; Awarded Pulitzer Prize

1923 Published *A Lost Lady*

1925 Published *The Professor's House*

1927 Published *Death Comes for the Archbishop*

1931 Published *Shadows on the Rock*

1947 Died Apr. 24 New York, N.Y.

CARRIE CHAPMAN CATT

Susan B. Anthony's successor as leader of the women's suffrage movement in America, Carrie Chapman Catt directed the national effort through the first two decades of the 20th century and led the final drive for ratification of the Federal amendment.

Carrie Lane worked her way through college. At twenty-two she became a high-school principal, at twenty-four one of the first women superintendents. After her husband, Leo Chapman, died, she worked with the Iowa Woman Suffrage Association and, in 1890, attended the first convention of the National American Woman Suffrage Association. Her marriage to George Catt included a contract ensuring her four months a year for suffrage work. His death left her financially independent.

Mrs. Catt's executive ability made her a valuable assistant to the aging Susan Anthony. As chairman of the NAWSA's Organization Committee, she established new branches and increased membership. An effective speaker, she campaigned extensively. When Miss Anthony retired, Mrs. Catt became president.

Mrs. Catt turned the NAWSA's efforts more toward political action, emphasizing participation in town meetings, caucuses, etc. Workshops in organizational and political techniques were established. She aligned the organization with the progressive movement and brought Jane Addams and other reformers into suffrage work. When she resigned in 1904, she left the NAWSA a far more professionally managed organization.

After Mr. Catt's death, she divided her suffrage efforts between New York state and international movements. In New York she organized a Woman Suffrage Party and, in 1917, helped win the vote for women in New York. She organized and led the International Woman Suffrage Alliance; when she retired, affiliates had increased from nine countries to thirty-two.

Mrs. Catt's successes led the NAWSA to draft her to return to the presidency. During her absence, Alice Paul had formed the Congressional Committee of NAWSA, a militant group which, in 1916, became the independent Woman's Party. Totally dedicated to the Federal amendment, Paul's group embraced the principle that the party in power must bear responsibility for Congress's failure to act. Mrs. Catt proposed her "Winning Plan," which combined lobbying for a Federal amendment with efforts to win in individual States — by constitutional referendum, by legislative action granting woman suffrage for presidential elections, and by gaining the right to vote in primaries. She believed that Congressional support for the Federal amendment could, in part, be won through the States.

Mrs. Catt conducted an educational campaign to sustain interest during the war. Although she had founded the Woman's Peace Party, she encouraged women's support of the war effort. After Congress passed the amendment, Mrs. Catt worked for ratification, which came in August 1920.

With ratification, Mrs. Catt founded the League of Women Voters. Her last major project was the Women's Centennial Exposition 1840-1940, honoring distinguished women in 100 professions not open to women in 1840.

1859   Born Jan. 9 Ripon, Wis.

1880   Graduated from Iowa State College

1881-83   School Principal, Mason City, Iowa

1883   School Superintendent, Mason City, Iowa

1885   Married Leo Chapman; died 1886

1890   Married George W. Catt; died 1905

1900-04   President, National American Women's Suffrage Assoc.

1902   Helped found International Woman Suffrage Alliance

1915   Founded Woman's Peace Party (With Jane Addams)

1915-20   President, National American Woman's Suffrage Assoc.

1920   Helped found League of Women Voters

1947   Died Mar. 9 New Rochelle, N.Y.

37

DOROTHY DAY

She was arrested and beaten for picketing on behalf of suffrage in 1917 — one of eight times she was jailed. Women's suffrage, prison reform, racial justice, fair wages, disarmament — all were causes to which Dorothy Day devoted herself with uncompromising commitment. A journalist and Catholic convert, she founded the Catholic worker movement, *The Catholic Worker* newspaper, and Houses of Hospitality for the homeless poor, and for five decades, largely through these instruments, she served those without jobs, food or shelter in cities throughout America.

Dorothy Day's father was a sports' writer and editor who moved frequently — from Brooklyn to Oakland, California, to Chicago, where Dorothy attended high school. At the University of Illinois her reading of Kropotkin, Upton Sinclair and others stimulated her interest in social justice. She joined the Socialist Party, moved to New York, and worked as a reporter for the Socialist *Call,* then the radical *The Masses.* Her experience in jail in Washington — for picketing the White House — sharpened her concern for the down-trodden. She worked as a nurse in a Brooklyn hospital, then returned to reporting. In Chicago, while working for a Communist newspaper, she lived with a Catholic family and began to learn about Catholicism.

She entered into a common-law marriage with Forster Batterham, a professed atheist, and it was the birth of their child, in 1927, which drew her to Catholicism. Near the end of 1927 she left Batterham and joined the Catholic Church.

In December 1932 Dorothy Day met Peter Maurin, a French-born Catholic layman who had developed a program of social action which included bringing scholars, workers and the needy together in houses of hospitality, farming communes and roundtable discussions. A newspaper would be their voice, their clarion. In May 1933 they published the first issue of *The Catholic Worker.* The penny-a-copy paper, which was sold on street corners by activists young and old, addressed such social problems as unemployment, working conditions and race relations. Within four months the circulation reached 25,000, by the end of 1933, 100,000. It was the depth of the Depression; the unemployed appeared at their door, and the first House of Hospitality was born. As *The Catholic Worker* carried the message of their work across the nation, other Houses of Hospitality sprang up. Dorothy Day traveled from city to city visiting Houses of Hospitality, living and working with the poor and writing articles on labor relations, strikes, etc. for her newspaper.

Influence of *The Catholic Worker* increased; its circulation reached 150,000. The newspaper was, in large measure, the voice of Dorothy Day: as editor and publisher she established the editorial policy and wrote most editorials. An unyielding advocate of pacificism, she maintained that position during World War II. In 1955 she led demonstrations against New York's civil defense drill — and was jailed. As in the rest of her life, she was, by her actions, giving ultimate testimony to her beliefs.

BY ED LETTAU

1897 Born Nov. 8 New York, N.Y.

1914-16 Attended University of Illinois

1916-17 Reporter for the *Call*

1917 Reporter for *The Masses*

1918-19 Nurse, King's County Hospital, N.Y.

1925 Married (common law) Forster Batterham

1933 Founded *The Catholic Worker* (with Peter Maurin) and Hospitality House

1938 Published *From Union Square to Rome*

1939 Published *Houses of Hospitality*

1948 Published *On Pilgrimage*

1952 Published *The Long Lonliness*

1960 Published *Thérèse*

1980 Died Nov. 29 New York, N.Y.

EMILY DICKINSON

America's greatest woman poet — the verdict many critics and scholars reached after they read hundreds of poems Emily Dickinson had written but never published during her lifetime. Once in print, her poems won a growing audience and she was recognized as a major American poet.

Emily was the second of three children of Edward and Emily Dickinson. Her father, a lawyer, was a pillar of the church and of the community — treasurer of Amherst College, a member of the Temperance Association, the Governor's Council, the Massachusetts legislature and, for a term, the United States Congress. A devoted but stern parent, he dominated the Dickinson home and, to a startling degree, his children's lives. Neither daughter married or left home for long; the son, when married, lived in the house next door.

Emily left home so few times that each departure was An Event. Her longest absence was her stay at Mount Holyoke Female Seminary in South Hadley, near Amherst, where she spent an unhappy year. She visited Boston several times and, in 1854, when her father was serving in Congress, she visited Washington. On a stop in Philadelphia she heard — and may have met — Reverend Charles Wadsworth, a married minister whose relationship with her has never been precisely established. She may have fallen in love with him, and he with her, but their correspondence was not preserved; hence there is scant evidence that he was the object of her love poems and, perhaps, the primary cause of her continued withdrawal from the world.

There were other men in her life. Benjamin Newton, a law student with her father's firm between 1847 and 1849, was, she wrote, "a gentle, yet grave Preceptor," but he died a few years later. Thomas Wentworth Higginson, a critic, became her literary advisor; he thought her poems "too delicate" for publication. Late in life Emily became deeply attached to Judge Otis Lord, a family friend. She was almost fifty, he sixty-six.

The portrait opposite is one of the few extant. Of herself Emily wrote: "I am small, like the Wren, and my hair is bold, like the Chestnut Bur — and my eyes, like the Sherry in the Glass, that the Guest leaves."

Emily Dickinson's quiet life was filled with family routine and household chores — invested with drama and mystery by a soaring imagination, acute sensibility, and poetic gift. She played the piano, baked bread, cultivated flowers and walked her dog. In her room she read — and wrote poems. "There is no Frigate like a Book/To take us Lands away/ Nor any Courses like a Page/ Of prancing Poetry."

Seven poems were published during her lifetime. There are 1775 poems in the variorum edition, revealing astonishing variety and power. Many embody the form and meter of hymns — adapted to the poet's distinctive needs; most glow with language that is spare and fresh. Her poetic techniques — and the range and depth of her thought — anticipate 20th century developments in poetry.

1830   Born Dec. 10 Amherst, Mass.

1847   Graduated from Amherst College

1847-48   Attended Mount Holyoke Female
         Seminary

1886   Died May 15 Amherst, Mass.

1890 ⎫
1891 ⎬ *Poems* (Selected) published
1896 ⎭

1924   *Complete Poems of Emily Dickinson*
       published

DOROTHEA DIX

Chaining "lunatics" in America's jails was, tragically, customary until Dorothea Dix made it her business to change it. Shy, with a tubercular condition but an iron will, she became one of America's most successful social reformers.

Young Dorothea was raised, in turn, by an invalid mother, a stern grandmother, and a kindly great aunt; her moral fervor was kindled and given direction by William Ellery Channing, a Unitarian minister concerned above all with social problems.

Largely self-educated, Dorothea opened a school for young girls, as well as a charity school, in Boston. She wrote books for children — a compilation of facts, *Conversations . . .* , and a collection of hymns. Her commitment to serve was total, and she drove herself to exhaustion and, eventually, illness, forcing complete rest — a pattern frequently repeated. In 1836, severely ill, she went to England: in eighteen months at the estate of William Rathbone, a friend of Channing's, she regained her strength and met social reformers like Robert Owen and Samuel Tuke, whose father had established in York a humane retreat for the mentally ill.

On March 28, 1841, while serving as substitute teacher for a Sunday-school class at the East Cambridge jail, Miss Dix discovered "lunatics" locked in filthy, unheated cages. Her indignation launched her on a lifelong crusade. She learned from Horace Mann and others that attempts at reform had largely been ignored; a thorough survey of every town and hamlet in the State was needed — to establish the facts. At 39, with a small private income, Dorothea Dix decided to conduct such a survey on her own — probably the first piece of social research in America.

After eighteen months of solitary travel to every jail and almshouse in the State, Miss Dix wrote a memorial for the State legislature. "I . . . call your attention," she wrote, "to the present state of Insane Persons confined within this Commonwealth, in *cages, closets, cellars, stalls, pens! Chained, naked, beaten with rods, and lashed into obedience!"* There were shocking facts, and recommendations. The facts were questioned; she was denounced for meddling, but reformers and some doctors supported her, and the bill was finally passed.

Dorothea Dix carried her crusade to other States — New York; Rhode Island, where she persuaded a Scrooge-like millionaire to donate $40,000; New Jersey, where she established the State's first mental hospital; Pennsylvania; Maryland; Kentucky and others. Her approach was the same: a careful survey, a "memorial" with compelling facts for the legislature, and patient personal lobbying. She used the press effectively, to educate the public and legislatures, sometimes to shame them to act. Success followed success. Then, in 1854-57, she traveled to England and the Continent, investigating conditions in jails, visiting new hospitals and, as always, recommending improvements.

The Civil War brought her first official post — as superintendent of Army nurses. The dauntless, somewhat imperious crusader proved a poor administrator. Afterwards, she continued her crusade, with further success: in 1841 there were 11 mental hospitals in the United States; in 1880, 123.

1802	Born Apr. 4 Hampden, Me.
1821-24 1831-36 }	Operated girls' school, Boston
1824	Published *Conversations on Common Things*
1832	Published *American Moral Tales for Young Persons*

1841-43	Conducted survey of Massachusetts jails
1845	Published *Remarks on Prisons & Prison Discipline in United States*
1861-66	Superintendent, U.S. Army Nurses
1887	Died Jul. 18 Trenton, N.J.

ISADORA DUNCAN

"Duncan was the greatest American gift to the art of the dance," —Michel Fokine, choreographer. A free spirit in art and life, Isadora Duncan dazzled the world with unique expressive dancing marked by natural simplicity and grace. Her greatest performances, drawing upon music and the graphic arts, such as the forms of classical sculpture, introduced entirely new concepts to the dance, carrying it to unprecedented heights as a creative art.

Isadora grew up in comparative poverty with little supervision. Her mother, who taught piano, encouraged Isadora, her sister and two brothers to play act and dance. At 6, Isadora was teaching other children to dance; at 12, she was performing before local audiences.

Experience acting and dancing with a New York theatrical company proved unsatisfying, and Isadora began to give solo performance in wealthy homes. In 1900 in London she achieved a critical success: performing in the court of an art gallery, she danced to classical themes, including a musical poem of Mendelssohn's, wearing a costume of gauze-like robes copied from Botticelli's "Primavera." A critic noted her "perfectly artless and natural dance movements," adding, "the whole dance seems like something that might have happened in ancient Greece." In Paris, her dancing at private parties, accompanied at times by Maurice Ravel, impressed the literati and artists, but it was not until her formal debut in 1902 in a Budapest theater that she scored a major triumph. In Munich, after her performances enthusiastic students unhitched the horses from her carriage and pulled it to her hotel. Greater triumphs followed at Berlin's Opera House. To the Germans she became *die Göttliche*.

Isadora's free-flowing dance symbolized her approach to life. In Budapest she had her first affair — with a Hungarian actor; in Berlin she began an intense affair with stage designer Gordon Craig. Her liaison with Paris Eugene Singer, heir to the sewing-machine fortune whom she met in Paris in 1909, lasted for years. In 1922 she married a young Russian poet, Sergei Yessenin.

Highlights of Duncan's career were performances at the Metropolitan Opera house with the New York Symphony Orchestra (1908) and at the Gaieté-Lyrique Theater in Paris (1909). Her performances in Russia influenced ballet, giving, according to one critic, "new life to the unalterable canons of classical ballet."

Ironically, Isadora, who believed in Walt Whitman's America and considered herself the embodiment of America's freedom, achieved her greatest triumphs before European audiences. In her art — and life — she pushed beyond the bonds of convention, at that time behavior more accepted in Europe. In the dance, her originality — improvisations distinctly her own — represented new modes of artistic expression, but the freedom in which she gloried — the absence of set movements — kept her art essentially a personal phenomenon. She brought to the dance not steps or patterns, but a liberating spirit and a sense of the unity of all the arts.

Duncan was killed instantly when her shawl caught in the spokes of a wheel of the Bugatti sports car in which she was riding.

1878   Born May 27 San Francisco, Calif.

1896-98 Actress, dancer, Augustin Daly's
        Company

1900   London debut, New Gallery

1905   Russian tour

1908   American tour

1916   South American tour

1922   Married Sergei Yessenin

1927   Died Sep. 14 Nice, France

AMELIA EARHART

Amelia Earhart was the first woman of flight — with an array of first's unmatched in the world. Her daring flights in the 1920s and 1930s captured the imagination of the American public and signaled that women could participate fully in pioneering this new frontier.

As a child, Amelia Earhart liked to ride horseback and a miniature home-made roller coaster. After high school, she tried nursing and premedical studies before she first flew — with barnstormer Frank Hawks in Glendale, California, in 1920. Two years later she was flying her own Kinner Canary in California air shows.

Amelia Earhart was working in a settlement house in Boston and flying in her free time when publisher George Putnam chose her to fly as a passenger on a transatlantic flight a year after Lindberg's historic crossing. Wilmer Stultz piloted the Fokker trimotor from Newfoundland to Wales; Amelia Earhart kept the flight log. She was the first woman to cross the Atlantic by air, and suddenly she was famous. New York gave "Lady Lindy" a ticker-tape parade. In 1931 Miss Earhart married George Putnam — with an agreement that she have complete freedom to travel. Putnam managed her affairs.

On May 21-22, 1932, Amelia Earhart flew solo from Newfoundland to Ireland. In a Lockheed monoplane she flew the 2026 miles in 14 hours, 56 minutes, much of it through storms and fog — the first woman to fly the Atlantic alone. She was smothered with honors — among others, the cross of the French Legion of Honor and the U.S. Distinguished Flying Cross. Other first's followed: two transcontinental records and the first non-stop flight from Mexico City to New York.

In 1937 a round-the-world flight (another first) was planned, to test long-range performance of crew and aircraft. After an unsuccessful attempt, on June 1st Amelia Earhart and navigator Fred Noonan left Miami, Florida, flying east on an equatorial route that took them across the Atlantic Ocean, Africa, and the Indian Ocean. At Lae, New Guinea, on July 2, they took off to fly 2570 miles to Howland Island, a spot in the Pacific scarcely longer than its runway. They never reached it. Hours after they were due, the Coast Guard cutter *Itaska*, near Howland, received their last voice messages: "...gas is running low..." and "We are on a line of position . . . ." Sea and air searches found nothing.

For years rumors persisted that Miss Earhart had been on an espionage mission and might have been captured by the Japanese. But the facts strongly suggest that the plane simply missed Howland and crashed into the sea.

Amelia Earhart had a passion for flying — she even wrote verse about it — but she was also deeply committed to the cause of feminism: both as a woman and a flyer, she was a pioneer. She once confided to her husband that, for her, the ideal way to die would be swiftly to go down with her plane.

1897   Born Jul. 24 Atchison, Kan.

1917-18   Red Cross Volunteer, Spadina Hospital, Canada

1919-20   Attended Columbia University

1926-28   Social worker, Denison House, Boston, Mass.

1928   Jun. 17-18 Flew (passenger), Newfoundland to Wales

1928   Published *20 Hrs. 40 mins.*

1931   Married George Putnam

1932   May 21-22 Flew solo, Newfoundland to Ireland

1932   Published *The Fun Of It*

1935   Flew solo, Honolulu to U.S. mainland (First)

1937   Jun. 1 Began round-the-world flight

1937   Jul. 2 Disappeared on flight over Pacific

1937   *Last Flight* published

47

MARY BAKER EDDY

An inspiring teacher and advocate of mental healing, Mary Baker Eddy was the founder of the Church of Christ, Scientist. Her book *Science and Health*, which outlines the principles and practices of Christian Science, sold over 400,000 copies in her lifetime.

Mary Baker was the youngest child of a stern Calvinist farmer. She was comparatively frail, subject to frequent illness — chronic back trouble and paroxysmal attacks — which kept her home, where she was tutored by her brother. She composed verse and early professed a desire to be a writer.

In 1843 she married George Glover, a contractor, who took her to Charleston, S.C. His sudden death left her destitute — and pregnant. She returned home, gave birth to a son, but illness forced her to place him with a friend. Mary on occasion taught school, her verse and articles appeared in local newspapers, and she began studying mesmerism and clairvoyance. Her marriage to Daniel Patterson, an itinerant dentist, proved unfortunate: in his travels he earned little; she was alone, frequently ill. In seeking help she learned of Phineas Quimby, a clockmaker-turned-healer who had gained a reputation for his practice in Portland, Maine.

Phineas Quimby had a profound effect on Mary — and on her life. Under his care she burst into vigorous health; she wrote extravagant testimonials for the *Courier*, likening Quimby's healing to Christ's. She began to study Quimby's writings, learning enough about his principles of mental healing and the "science of health" to undertake, in time, the role of healer herself. Occasionally she lectured on "Quimby's spiritual science," and she was devastated when, in 1866, Quimby died. Shortly thereafter she fell on ice, injuring her back; a physician treated her, but she attributed her recovery to prayer.

From that time Mary devoted herself with new intensity to teaching — and developing — the principles of healing through faith and prayer. Separated — and later divorced — from Patterson, she lived with former Quimby disciples and others interested in spiritual healing, teaching and working on her manuscript, which was published as *Science and Health* in 1875. That year she established The Christian Scientists' Home in a house in Lynn, Massachusetts. Two years later she married one of her assistants, Asa Eddy.

With a growing group of followers, Mrs. Eddy preached every Sunday either in Lynn or Boston. Originally, the movement was not considered a formal religion, but in 1879 it was chartered as the Church of Christ (Scientist). At the Massachusetts Metaphysical College, which she founded in 1881, Mrs. Eddy conducted courses in her science of healing, in eight years teaching over 600 students, some of whom taught and practiced Christian Science elsewhere.

As new churches sprang up, several groups of members revolted, challenging Mrs. Eddy's methods and motives. Questions of authority were resolved when, in 1895, a centralized, controlling function was permanently established in the Mother Church in Boston. Besides the church, *The Christian Science Monitor* is part of the legacy of Mary Baker Eddy.

1821	Born Jul. 16 Bow, N.H.
1843	Married George Glover; died 1844
1853	Married Daniel Patterson; divorced 1873
1875	Published *Science and Health*
1876	Formed Christian Science Association
1877	Married Asa Eddy; died 1882

1879	Church of Christ (Scientist) chartered
1881	Founded Massachusetts Metaphysical College
1886	Founded National Christian Science Association
1908	Founded *Christian Science Monitor*
1910	Died Dec. 3 Brookline, Mass.

49

MARGARET FULLER

"I now know all the people worth knowing in America, and I find no intellect comparable to my own," Margaret Fuller once observed. An outspoken champion — and exemplar — of the cause of women, she was the most prominent woman in the intellectual circle in Boston that included Emerson and Thoreau. Her book *Woman in the Nineteenth Century* was the first detailed statement of feminism in America, inspiring the first women's rights convention at Seneca Falls, New York, in 1848.

The eldest child, Margaret was raised by her father, a lawyer and Harvard graduate, as if she were a son: he directed her study of English and Latin grammer; at seven she was reading Virgil and Ovid daily, later Cervantes, Moliere, the English novelists and Shakespeare. After two years of formal schooling, she resumed private study — of music, philosophy, German, French, Italian and Greek. At 18 she was recognized by Cambridge intellectuals as a prodigy — a captivating, sometimes intimidating, conversationalist.

After several years of isolation on the family farm, Margaret spent an intense year teaching at the progressive Temple School in Boston, operated by Bronson Alcott, father of author Louisa May. Margaret dazzled Alcott and the students, and won an offer of a less demanding job at a Providence school.

In 1839 Margaret returned to Boston — to be a tutor — and was caught up in the spirtual and philosophical ferment later labelled Transcendentalism. She joined Emerson, Alcott, Theodore Parker and George Ripley as a leader of this liberal, liberating movement that defied precise definition. The group turned to conversations — to debate, discuss, explore — and Margaret, whom Alcott called "the most commanding talker of the day, of her sex," organized formal Conversation for women.

Margaret Fuller's Conversations were undoubtedly her finest achievement: comments of participants suggest that at these meetings Margaret became a masterful teacher-philospher whose brilliant analyses and explanations cast a wondrous spell over the group, described by Emerson as "the most agreeable and intelligent women in Boston." Among them were the wives of Emerson, historian George Bancroft, and educator Horace Mann. Subjects covered included art, ethics, mythology, education, and women's rights. Margaret won a devoted following; the Conversations continued for five years, giving stimulus and stature to women's intellectual activities, serving as a model for future women's clubs, and developing ideas that appeared later in *Woman in the Nineteenth Century*.

Fuller's first published writing appeared in the *Dial*, a Transcendentalist quarterly. As literary critic for the *New York Tribune*, she produced some of her most distinguished writing. Editor Horace Greeley, whom called her, "in some respects the greatest woman whom America has yet known, " made her the *Tribune's* foreign correspondent.

In Europe Margaret Fuller met Wordsworth, George Sand, Chopin and the Italian patriot Mazzini — and became involved in the Italian revolution. She fell in love with Marchese d'Ossoli and bore him a son. Later they married. All three were lost when their ship was destroyed in a storm outside New York harbor.

1810 Born May 23 Cambridgeport, Mass.

1824-26 Attended Prescott's School, Groton, Mass.

1836-37 Teacher, Temple School, Boston Mass.

1837-39 Teacher, Green St. School, Providence, R.I.

1839-44 Conducted Conversations

1840-42 Editor, *The Dial*

1844-46 Critic, *New York Tribune*

1844 Published *Summer on the Lakes*

1845 Published *Woman in the Nineteenth Century*

1846 Published *Papers on Literature and Art*

1846- Foreign correspondent, *New York Tribune*

1849 Married Giovanni Angelo, Marchese d'Ossoli

1850 Died Jul. 19 Aboard *Elizabeth* in Atlantic storm

CHARLOTTE PERKINS GILMAN

Lecturer, author, feminist — Charlotte Perkins Gilman was one of the foremost intellectuals of the women's movement in America: her ideas on the economic independence of women gave generations of American women a vision of a new role in society.

Charlotte's father, Frederick Beecher Perkins — nephew of lecturer Henry Ward Beecher and Harriet Beecher Stowe — left his wife with two children and little support. They moved from relative to relative, Charlotte from school to school. She excelled in elocution. At 17, having resolved to "help humanity," she began her own program of study to prepare herself; later she devised exercises to develop rational behavior, self-discipline, honesty and other desired characteristics. Growth was the touchstone of her philosophy.

Charlotte turned to painting and teaching to support herself. After agonizing doubts, she married Charles Stetson, a painter. She soon fell into depression and, after the birth of her daughter, a deep melancholia. A trip, alone, to California brought speedy recovery and she remained separated. After they were divorced, Stetson married Charlotte's friend Grace Channing, and Charlotte, ever the idealist, challenged the conventional pieties by permitting her daughter to live with them — setting off a scandal.

In California Charlotte taught drawing, wrote articles and poems, and began lecturing. Satirical poems ridiculing prejudice and the closed mind — the enemies of growth — attracted notice. Influenced by the ideas of Edward Bellamy (whose utopian *Looking Backward* was published in 1888), she lectured on topics related to social reform, labor, and women to clubs, unions and church groups — in California and, as her reputation grew, throughout the nation. She visited Jane Addam's Hull House in Chicago, met the Fabians, G.B. Shaw and the Webbs in London. She was interested in socialism but was never a Socialist, rejecting Marxism.

Publication of *Women and Economics,* which advocated economic independence and a social role for women far beyond the demands of suffragists, brought Charlotte wider fame, sharper criticism. Some American suffragists saw her radical ideas endangering their cause. Controversial proposals — in 1898 — included centralized nurseries and cooperative kitchens, to free women from domestic duties. The book was published in England, Germany, and Hungary, and well as Russia and Japan.

In 1900 Charlotte married her cousin George Gilman, but she continued to write and to lecture. Her books *Concerning Children* and *The Home* developed the theme of the independent working woman; *Human Work* was an ambitious sociological treatise with a utopian view of human work. She founded — and wrote and published — a monthly magazine *Forerunner*: for seven years she produced fiction, poems, editorials and articles on women and social reform, a literary *tour de force* that she estimated equated to 28 books. In *Man-Made World* she argued that the male-dominated world of aggression could be changed if women, by nature peaceful and cooperative, played a larger role in society.

Charlotte Gilman's faith in social progress survived World War I. In her autobiography, she concluded: "This is the woman's century, the first chance for the mother of the world to rise to her full place . . . ."

1860	Born Jul. 3 Hartford, Ct.	1903	Published *The Home*
1876	Attended Rhode Island School of Design	1904	Published *Human Work*
1884	Married Charles Stetson; divorced 1894	1909-16	Editor and Publisher, *The Forerunner*
1893	Published *In This Our World* (Verse)	1911	Published *Man-Made World*
1898	Published *Women and Economics*	1915	Co-founder, Women's Peace Party
1900	Married George Gilman	1935	Published autobiography
1900	Published *Concerning Children*	1935	Died Aug. 17 Pasadena, Cal.

ANGELINA AND SARAH GRIMKE

"The ground upon which you stand is holy ground: never — never surrender it." Angelina Grimke wrote William Garrison, the abolitionist, in 1875 — words which Garrison published and which launched Angelina and her sister Sarah as the first women activists supporting abolition, the first actively seeking women's rights.

Born into an aristocratic, slave-holding family in South Carolina, the sisters both found slavery repugnant: they could not accept the cruelty and injustice they witnessed, nor reconcile their church's (Episcopal) acceptance of slavery with the Christian message. Both left Charleston and their church; by 1830 both were living in Philadelphia as members of the Society of Friends, engaged primarily in charitable work.

Angelina, the more independent, began to attend anti-slavery meetings; impressed by a lecture given by British abolitionist George Thompson, she joined the Philadelphia Female Anti-Slavery Society. News of mob violence against abolitionists in New York and Philadelphia moved Angelina to write to Garrison: in the face of such danger, she wrote, "this is a cause worth dying for . . . ." The letter was reprinted in other reform publications. Encouraged, she wrote *An Appeal to the Christian Women of the Southern States,* a bold appeal to women in the name of righteousness to help overthrow slavery; it helped the cause in the North, was publicly burned in the South. She could no longer return home.

Sarah, resenting Quaker discrimination against blacks, gradually adopted Angelina's views. The sisters were the first women to enlist with the American Anti-Slavery Society, talking before small groups of women in New York. A training course by abolitionist orator Theodore Weld sharpened their arguments and better prepared them for hostile audiences.

For almost two years (1837-38) Angelina and Sarah toured the East and New England lecturing in parlors, churches and town halls, occasionally to audiences of men and women. They visited over 60 towns, talked to over 40,000 people. In one town, Angelina debated two men who challenged her and, citing her own knowledge of slavery, demolished their arguments. Addressing mixed audiences produced a more fundamental challenge — a woman's *right* to do so. Some ministers challenged the sisters' right to address *any* public group. Angelina responded: "We have given great offense on account of our womanhood, which seems to be as objectionable as our abolitionism...We are willing to bear the brunt of the storm, if we can only be the means of making a break in the wall of public opinion which lies right in the way of women's rights, true dignity, honor and usefulness." She later wrote: "I believe it is woman's right to have a voice in all the laws and regulations by which she is governed," and Sarah expanded on this in *Letters on the Equality of the Sexes.*

After Angelina married Theodore Weld, the trio became less active, but they collaborated in compiling *American Slavery As It Is* — interviews and reports which documented the brandings, whippings and other barbarities suffered by American slaves, the most telling account published in America before *Uncle Tom's Cabin.*

ANGELINA GRIMKE

SARAH

1792 Born Nov. 26 Charleston, S.C.

1836 Published *Epistle to the Clergy of Southern States*

1837-38 New England lecture tour

1838 Odeon Lectures, Boston, Mass.

1838 Published *Letters on the Equality of the Sexes*

1839 Published *American Slavery As It Is* (Co-author)

1873 Died Dec. 23 Hyde Park, Mass.

ANGELINA

1805 Born Feb. 20 Charleston S.C.

1835 Published letter in *Liberator*

1836 Published *An Appeal to the Christian Women of the South*

1838- Odeon Lectures

1838 Married Theodore Weld

1839 Published *American Slavery At It Is* (Co-author)

1879 Died Oct. 26 Hyde Park, Mass.

SARAH HALE

She edited the most successful magazine in America in the mid-19th century — *Godey's Lady's Book*: for forty years Sarah Hale used this pulpit to fight for women's education, to advise women on everything from health and morals to household hints, and to instill in readers scattered throughtout a growing nation a sense of pride in things American, including its own literature.

Sarah Buell's mother taught her to read and together they studied the Bible and the works of Shakespeare, Milton and Bunyan. When her brother attended Dartmouth, he tutored her in the subjects he was studying. Sarah taught school and wrote verse for children. After she married lawyer David Hale, her housekeeping was balanced by regular evening reading of the classics. Hale died suddenly and Sarah opened a millinery shop and began writing for publication.

Her verses appeared in the *Spectator* and the *Ladies' Album*, a collection of them as *The Genius of Oblivion*. A novel contrasting life in the North and South, *Northwood*, was a success — and was published also in England. *Poems for Our Children* included the undying "Mary's Lamb."

Shortly after *Northwood* appeared, Sarah Hale became editor of the new *Ladies' Magazine*; "my first object was to promote the education of my sex," she wrote. She informed readers of the new women's "seminaries" established by Emma Willard and Mary Lyon, and advocated that the Government establish normal schools for women. The magazine reflected her high standards: she published only original pieces, many by women, and supported such worthy causes as raising funds for a Bunker Hill monument and establishing a Seaman's Aid Society for the widows and children of shipwrecked sailors.

When *Godey's Lady's Book* bought the *Ladies' Magazine* in 1837, Sarah Hale became editor of *Godey's*, which she promptly improved with original contributions, well-executed illustrations and fashion plates, and her own instructive comments. The creators of an American literature — Edgar Allen Poe, Ralph Waldo Emerson, Oliver Wendell Holmes and Nathaniel Hawthorne — were contributors. Poe's "The Cask of Amontillado" first appeared in *Godey's*. Sarah Hale counseled women to develop their own (American) taste in fashions, to exercise — by dancing, skating, riding, and to study and prepare themselves for their role as spiritual and intellectual force in the family; she did not advocate political equality with men or "this notion of female voting." Women reigned supreme in their sphere — in the home, although she later championed women's education for careers in medical and social work.

In 1860 *Godey's* circulation reached 150,000. Sarah Hale, ever the patriot, rallied these legions to support the preservation of Mt. Vernon as a national shrine and the establishment of Thanksgiving as a national holiday (Lincoln's Proclamation: 1863). Her editorials publicized the new Vassar College. At 89 she wrote her last editorial for *Godey's*. In addition to fifty years of poems, editorials and columns, she had written — or edited — over fifty books. *Woman's Record*, a collection of 2500 biographies "from the Creation to 1850," was republished several times and survives today.

1788   Born Oct. 24 Newport, N.H.

1813   Married David Hale

1823   Published *The Genius of Oblivion*

1827   Published *Northwood*

1828-37   Editor, *Ladies Magazine*

1830   Published *Poems for Our Children*

1833   Founded Seaman's Aid Society of Boston

1853   Published *Woman's Record*

1867   Published *Manners*

1879   Died Apr. 30 Philadelphia, Pa.

ALICE HAMILTON

Alice Hamilton practically created the field of industrial medicine in the United States: a physician and pathologist with exceptional credentials, she conducted the first surveys of the use — and effects — of poisons in American industries and helped develop controls to ensure proper protection of endangered workers. Her book *Industrial Poisons in the United States*, the first on the subject in America, publicized the dangers of industrial poisons and provided stimulus for the development and passage of workmen's compensation laws.

Tutored by her father, who loved the classics, Alice Hamilton had only two years of formal schooling before she began to study medicine. At American and German universities she acquired first-rate scientific and medical training, and was appointed professor of pathology at Northwestern's Woman's Medical School.

In Chicago Miss Hamilton became a resident at Jane Addam's Hull House; after teaching at the university, she would devote evenings to social work or classes for the poor. She remained at Hull House for twenty-two years, gaining experiences which shaped her career. During a typhoid epidemic in Chicago, her observations of life in the tenements led her to conclude that flies played an important role in spreading the contagion, and to write a paper that effected improvements in Health Department procedures. And it was in the Hull House neighborhood that she first learned of workers who had been permanently invalidated by breathing poisonous fumes in factories and mills. Pursuing the subject, she discovered that poisoning and other diseases were common in many American industries, and that no one — industry, government, or the medical profession — was doing anything about it. In Germany and England, she learned, industrial medicine was a recognized branch of medical science, and authorities had established effective systems for inspecting factories.

Dr. Hamilton found an ally in Professor Charles Henderson of the University of Chicago, who had studied German industrial insurance; he persuaded the Illinois governor to establish an Occupational Disease Commission. Dr. Hamilton was appointed to direct a State survey of industrial poisons; her findings led to the first State laws on occupational safety and workmen's compensation. Next she was appointed by the U.S. Commissioner of Labor to conduct nation-wide surveys of the uses of poisons in industry, and for the next ten years she — alone — carried on detailed investigations of the lead, mining and munitions industries. The cultivated, scholarly physician sought out the remote workrooms of factories where dust and fumes filled the air, and obtained samples for analysis, sometimes in the face of hostile owners who considered any interest in the welfare of workers as "socialism." Her carefully documented reports led to new safety laws and improved working conditions.

A pacifist, Alice Hamilton served with Jane Addams as a delegate to the 1915 peace meeting of the International Congress of Women at the Hague. In 1919 she became Harvard's first woman professor. Ultimately she won an international reputation as an expert on industrial diseases. Her accomplishments are modestly, and interestingly, presented in her autobiography, *Exploring the Dangerous Trade*.

1869   Born Feb. 27 New York, N.Y.

1893   Graduated from University of Michigan College of Medicine (MD)

1895-96   Attended University of Leipzig and University of Munich

1896-97   Attended Johns Hopkins Medical School

1897-1902   Professor of pathology, Womans' Medical School, Northwestern University

1902-11   Bacteriologist, Memorial Institute for Infectious Diseases

1910   Member, Illinois Commission on Occupational Diseases

1911-21   Special investigator, U.S. Bureau of Labor

1919-35   Assistant Professor, Harvard Medical School

1924-30   Member, Health Committee, League of Nations

1925   Published *Industrial Poisons in the U.S.*

1934   Published *Industrial Toxicology*

1942   Published *Exploring the Dangerous Trades*

1970   Died Sep. 22 Hadlyme, Conn.

JULIA WARD HOWE

It was autumn 1861. Union troops were marching near Washington singing "John Brown's Body" as they swung past the waiting carriage. Julia Howe and her friends watched the soldiers and sang. Rev. James Clarke urged Mrs. Howe to write fresh words for that tune. That night she awoke and scribbled the words as they came: "Mine eyes have seen the glory...." She had been writing verse all her life, but this time she struck flint: her verse, with its Biblical echoes, became indeed "The Battle Hymn of the Republic."

Daugther of a New York banker with strict religious views, Julia Ward was educated by governesses and tutors. She was a bright, earnest student: she read *Pilgrim's Progress* at age nine, at twelve was writing religious verse. She studied French, German and Italian — and became a life-long student of German literature and philosophy. She published several literary articles.

After her father's death, Julia blossomed in New York society. Her marriage to Dr. Samuel Howe took her to Boston, where he headed the Perkins Institution. At 42, Howe was internationally known as the hero of Greece's struggle for independence and the developer of the method for teaching language to a blind deaf mute (Laura Bridgman). Dynamic but domineering, he did not encourage Julia's literary efforts: she was to be a mother and housewife. She raised their six children, escaped to Europe for one year — on her inheritance, and wrote verses limning their strained relationship.

The oft-published Battle Hymn brought Julia celebrity that ultimately far exceeded her husband's; thus launched into the world, she embraced a public life that centered on the cause of women. She helped found the New England Woman's Suffrage Association; for years she was president of the Massachusetts Woman's Suffrage Association, and when Lucy Stone broke with Susan B. Anthony, Julia helped Stone establish the American Woman's Suffrage Association. With Stone, she founded and for years edited the *Woman's Journal*.

Convinced that women should participate in the cultural and social, as well as political world, Julia Howe became one of the leading supporters of the women's club movement. She served for many years as president of the New England Women's Club and helped establish the Assocation for the Advancement of Women — concerned with participation in the professions — and the General Federation of Women's Clubs, both national organizatons.

An engaging, witty — sometimes caustic — speaker, Julia Howe lectured extensively, touring the Midwest in 1876, the West Coast in 1888. She was a missionary for the causes of women, culture and peace: she urged women to participate fully in society, denounced the crassness and materialism of the times, and championed the oppressed peoples of Europe. She was the first president of the United Friends of Armenia.

Still active in her eighties, Julia Ward Howe became an American institution. The first woman elected to the American Academy of Arts and Letters, she was, to the adoring public, the "Dearest old Lady in America."

BEGUN BY J. ELLIOTT
FINISHED BY WILLIAM COTTEN

NATIONAL PORTRAIT GALLERY
SMITHSONIAN INSTITUTION

1819   Born May 27 New York, N.Y.

1843   Married Samuel Gridley Howe

1854   Published *Passion Flowers* (Verse)

1857   Published *Words for the Hours* (Verse)

1862   "Battle Hymn of the Republic" published in *Atlantic Monthly*

1868-77   President, New England Woman's Suffrage Assoc.

1870-78   President, Massachusetts Woman's Suffrage Assoc.

1871   President, New England Women's Club

1873   Helped found Association for Advancement of Women

1883   Published biography of Margaret Fuller

1893-98   Director, General Federation of Women's Clubs

1900   Published *Reminiscences*

1908   First woman elected to American Academy of Arts & Letters

1910   Died Oct. 17 Newport, R.I.

HELEN KELLER

"I feel that in this child I have seen more of the Divine than has been manifest in anyone I ever met before" — Alexander Graham Bell. "My children understand her . . . . But the children of the future will understand her even better, for they will be liberated and will know how the spirit can prevail over the senses" — Maria Montessori. "She is fellow to Caesar, Alexander, Napoleon, Homer, Shakespeare and the rest of the immortals. She will be as famous a thousand years from now as she is today" — Mark Twain.

At 19 months, Helen Keller permanently lost her sight and hearing when struck by a mysterious illness. She became wild, unreachable. Alexander G. Bell recommended the Perkins Institution in Boston, which had developed a method that had succeeded with deaf-blind Laura Bridgman. A recent Perkins graduate, Anne Sullivan, 20, accepted the challenge. At the Keller home, the strong-willed Sullivan won the child's affection and obedience, constantly striving to teach her the manual alphabet. Within a month she succeeded — at the dramatic moment when Helen, at the water pump, felt the water on one hand, the letters W-A-T-E-R on the other. " I left the well house eager to learn," Helen later wrote. "As we returned to the house every object which I touched seemed to quiver with life."

Once the door was opened, Helen could not learn enough. She learned to write, and Helen and Teacher (Miss Sullivan) went joyously from subject to subject. With Teacher, Helen studied at Cambridge School for Young Ladies and at Radcliffe College. With the aid of Miss Sullivan and Harvard instructor John Macy, Helen wrote her autobiography *The Story of My Life*. The book was a startling revelation of the rich life Helen had achieved in spite of the blunted senses; it was widely publicized and favorably reviewed — "unique in the world of literature."

After graduation, Helen and Teacher settled in Wrentham, Massachusetts. Anne Sullivan married John Macy, with the understanding Helen was her permanent charge. Anne and John Macy helped Helen with her next book, *The World I Live In*. Again, a success.

Helen actively supported the cause of the blind and women's suffrage; she became a socialist, writing tracts on social justice; with Teacher she made lecture tours across the country. In 1913 John Macy separated from Anne; the next year Polly Thompson joined Helen and Teacher as secretary and housekeeper.

Helen's world continued to expand. She participated in peace rallies; she lectured, appeared in vaudeville, made a movie. She traveled extensively raising funds for the American Foundation for the Blind; she lobbied in Washington. After Anne Sullivan died (1936), Polly Thompson became Helen's interpreter and companion. They visited military hospitals during World War II and made a world tour for the cause of the blind.

Now a world figure, Helen Keller was the subject of another movie, *The Unconquered,* and a play, *The Miracle Worker* — attempts to document a life that testified to the unfathomable reaches of the human spirit.

1880	Born June 27 Tuscumbia, Ala.	1913	Published *Out of the Dark*
1887-	Studied under Anne Sullivan	1927	Published *My Religion*
1903	Published *The Story of My Life*	1929	Published *Midstream*
1904	Graduated from Radcliffe College	1938	Published *Helen Keller's Journal*
1906-	Member, Massachusetts Commission for the Blind	1955	Published *Teacher*
1909	Published *The World I Live In*	1968	Died June 1 Westport, Ct.

DOROTHEA LANGE

"An extraordinary phenomenon in photography," Ansel Adams called her: "she is both a humanitarian and an artist . . . . Her pictures are both records of actuality and exquisitively sensitive emotional documents." Dorothea Lange was America's foremost documentary photographer; her photographs of victims of the Depression created a new genre and at the same time set an almost impossible standard for others. The powerful images she recorded helped bring government aid to impoverished communities.

When Dorothea Lange graduated from high school, she was determined to become a photographer. She took teacher training — to satisfy her mother — but worked afternoons for professional photographers, learning techniques and gaining experience, and attended Clarence White's photography course at Columbia University.

Lange moved to San Francisco, worked briefly for a photographer, and then opened her own studio. Members of prosperous families sought her soft-focus portraits, and her business prospered. She met and married the painter Maynard Dixon; both continued their careers. Dorothea visited Indian reservations with Dixon — and her camera, and took unposed pictures of the forgotten Indians, some of her earliest experiments in documentary photography.

During the first years of the Depression, Lange's portrait business diminished but continued, but, as the situation worsened, she became more interested in subjects outside of her studio. "The discrepancy between what I was working on in the printing frames and what was going on in the street was more than I could assimilate," she later observed. In 1932 she took several photographs of a bread line near her studio; "White Angel Bread Line" — showing an unshaven, broken man, his back turned to the other — became, in time, what her biographer called "one of the great images of the Depression," her first outstanding documentary.

An exhibit of her documentary photographs in Oakland brought Lange and economist Paul Taylor together. Deeply interested in labor problems, Taylor had used a camera in field work. He recognized Lange's talent and they became a team, documenting conditions of migrant laborers for the California Emergency Relief Administration. Their reports — her captioned photographs and his text — helped obtain government funds to build decent camps for migrants. Officials acknowledged the impact of her powerful pictures. She began working for the U.S. Resettlement Administration, covering the West.

On her first field trip, Lange photographed "Migrant Mother," capturing the depths of care and anxiety on the face of a raggedly clothed woman with her three grimy children — a profoundly human picture that was published and exhibited throughout the world, ultimately becoming one of the best-known American photographs. This and other photographs of migrants documented the great social upheaval of the Thirties; some were published with Archibald MacLeish's poem Land of the Free, some in the more comprehensive book she did with Taylor, An American Exodus, a unique documentary where pictures did far more than simply illustrate the text.

Lange continued to photograph the American scene with telling effect. "If any documents of this turbulent age are justified to endure, Ansel Adams wrote, "the photographs of Dorothea Lange shall, most certainly."

THE DOROTHEA LANGE COLLECTION
THE OAKLAND MUSEUM

1895 Born May 26 Hoboken, N.J.

1914-17 Attended New York Training School for Teachers

1920 Married Maynard Dixon; divorced 1935

1934 First exhibit, Van Dyke Gallery, Oakland, Cal.

1935 Married Paul Taylor

1935- Photographer, U.S. Resettlement Administration

1939 Published *An American Exodus: A Record of Human Erosion* (With Paul Taylor)

1941-42 Guggenheim Fellow

1965 Died Oct. 11 San Francisco, Cal.

MARY LYON

"Beyond any woman I have ever known, she was a woman of ideas and principles," Amherst Professor William Tyler declared at the fiftieth anniversary of Mount Holyoke College, "and she became the founder of this institution simply as a means of incorporating and perpetuating them." By establishing a school with independent support, a board of trustees, a permanent campus and buildings, and a college curriculum, Mary Lyon — expanding on the work of Emma Willard — created an institution of higher learning for women that would endure and serve as a model for others.

At school young Mary Lyon demonstrated a quick mind and a thirst for knowledge. She mastered Alexander's *English Grammar* in four days, a Latin grammar in three. She combined teaching with study at Sanderson Academy. At a local school she introduced the idea of coloring maps, memorialized in: "Geography was too abstruse/ Till Mary Lyon taught its use."

Reverend Joseph Emerson, head of Byfield Seminary, helped give direction and purpose to the young teacher who, at 24, attended Byfield. Educated at Harvard and Cambridge, Emerson had established his school to provide first-rate education for women preparing to teach; he believed that women at home and school should transmit culture, and he advocated the establishment of permanent educational institutions for women. Impressed by his theories, Mary Lyon later chose his favorite Biblical text, "That our daughters may be as cornerstones, polished after the similitude of a palace," as the motto of Mount Holyoke.

An inspired Mary Lyon returned to teaching at Sanderson. Then she started a girl's school in Buckland, which proved successful; summers she taught at Adams Female Academy in New Hampshire, established by Zilpah Grant, who had been preceptress at Byfield. Miss Grant fell out with the Adams' trustees, and she and Mary Lyon tried to establish a permanent school in Ipswich, Massachusetts; it failed for lack of support.

Obsessed with the idea of a permanent school for women, Mary Lyon devised her own plan: an institution of higher learning with its own land, supported by the public and managed by trustees, with board and tuition at cost, housework performed by students, and dedicated teachers on reduced salaries. In September 1834 she met with a committee who undertook to raise funds. From door to door, town to town Mary Lyon solicited the first $1000 needed to finance the fund-raising; over $27,000 was finally raised — from some 1800 people in 91 towns. After South Hadley, Massachusetts, was selected, nearby Mount Holyoke provided the name. In 1836 the institution was chartered and construction started, all under Mary Lyon's guiding hand.

Eighty students converged on Mount Holyoke's substantial brick building in November 1837 to begin a three-year course of study based on the Amherst College curriculum. The next year 400 applicants were turned away. Mary Lyon directed the college and continued to teach until her death in 1849. By then both Mount Holyoke and the principle of higher education for women were securely established.

BY JOSEPH CHANDLER

MOUNT HOLYOKE COLLEGE ART COLLECTION

1797 Born Feb. 28 Buckland, Mass.

1814 Taught summer school

1817- Attended Sanderson Academy, Ashfield, Mass.

1821 Attended Byfield Female Seminary, Byfield, Mass.

1824- Taught at Adams Female Academy, Londonderry, N.H.

1837 Founded Mount Holyoke Female Seminary

1843 Published *A Missionary Offering*

1849 Died Mar. 5 South Hadley, Mass.

MARGARET MEAD

America's foremost woman anthropologist, Margaret Mead authored scientific studies of primitive societies that made anthropology meaningful to an unprecedented number of American readers. *Coming of Age in Somoa* and *Growing Up in New Guinea* both ranked as national best sellers; these and other studies introduced Americans to cultures where male and female roles differed markedly from those in Western society and where adolescence was practically free of trauma and rebellion.

Margaret Mead's parents were both scholars — Edward Mead, an economist; Emily, a sociologist. Margaret's paternal grandmother, a former teacher and psychologist, taught her — by age 8 — to observe, and take notes on, the behavior of younger children. In her adolescence, at DePauw University, Margaret experienced the cruelty of exclusion from the North American tribal system called sororities. At Barnard College she was influenced by Professors Franz Boaz and Ruth Benedict to pursue the study of anthropology

Margaret Mead's first field expedition took her to the island of Tau, Samoa. There she immersed herself in village life, learned the language, and through interviews and observation gathered the material that became her first book. Called "a remarkable contribution to our knowledge of humanity." the book was reprinted five times in two years. Her next research, conducted in the Admiralty Islands in collaboration with her husband, anthropologist Reo Fortune, produced the study of primitive children *Growing Up in New Guinea.* On her second trip to New Guinea Mead studied the "conditioning of the social personalities of the two sexes" in three contrasting tribes — Arapesh, Mundugumor, and Tchambuli; her study *Sex and Temperament in Three Primitive Societies* won the praise of critics and scientists.

After her return, Margaret Mead divorced Reo Fortune and soon after married Gregory Bateson, British anthropologist she had met in New Guinea. Their extensive field work in Bali yielded *Balinese Character,* a book incorporating a revoluntionary use of photographs (over 700) to document behavior.

Mead's dramatic accomplishments brought recognition: her first honorary degree (D.Sc. from Wilson College, Chambersburg, Pa.), a visiting professorship at Vassar, a gold medal from the Society for Women Geographers, and, ironically, the Chi Omega sorority's achievement award.

During World War II she wrote pamphlets for the Government and served as advisor on intercultural and mental health problems, and as executive secretary of the committee on food habits of the National Research Council. After the war she taught at Columbia and wrote *Male and Female: A Study of the Sexes in a Changing World,* in which she applied insights gained in the Pacific to her own culture. One conclusion she reached: "Differences in sex as they are known today . . . are based on the bringing up by the mother."

Over the years Margaret Mead became a national institution; she wrote over thirty books and lectured widely. Of her profession she concluded (in her autobiography): "There is hope, I believe, in seeing the human adventure as a whole and in the shared trust that knowledge about mankind, sought in reverence for life, can bring life."

1901	Born Dec. 16 Philadelphia, Pa.
1919-20	Attended DePauw University
1923	Married Luther Cressman; divorced 1927
1923	Graduated from Barnard College
1924	Received MA from Columbia University
1926-	Assistant Curator, American Museum of Natural History
1928	Married Reo Fortune; divorced 1935
1928	Published *Coming of Age in Samoa*
1929	Received PHD from Columbia University

1930	Published *Growning Up in New Guinea*
1935	Published *Sex and Temperament in Three Primitive Societies*
1936	Married Gregory Bateman
1939-41	Visiting Professor, Vassar College
1941	Published *Balinese Character: A Photographic Analysis*
1949	Published *Male and Female*
1947-51	Visiting Professor, Teachers' College, Columbia University
1972	Published autobiography, *Blackberry Winter*
1978	Died Nov. 15 New York, N.Y.

EDNA ST. VINCENT MILLAY

In the Roaring Twenties Edna St. Vincent Millay was America's most popular woman poet: her cynical, witty verse caught the spirit of the times, her independent life symbolized it. The first poem in *A Few Figs* . . . (1920) opens: "My candle burns at both ends;/ It will not last the night;/ But ah, my foes, and oh, my friends —/ It gives a lovely light." Her best poems — about love, nature, beauty — reach beyond this, winning her a secure place as a lyric poet.

Edna's divorced mother Cora raised her to be independent and creative: at home, Edna read Shakespeare, Milton and Tennyson, wrote poems and studied piano. At 14, she saw her first poem published — in *St. Nicholas Magazine.*

"Renascence," published in the anthology *Lyric Year* in 1912, brought Edna recognition and a college scholarship. At Vassar she studied literature and languages, flaunted regulations, composed poems, and wrote and acted in school plays. Although committed to poetry, upon graduation she turned to the theater for a job — to Greenwich Village and the Provincetown Players. She acted in several plays and, as "Nancy Boyd," wrote poems and stories for popular magazines like *Ainslee's.* Her world of Village writers and revoluntionaries included Edmund Wilson, Max Eastman, Floyd Dell and John Reed. Publication of *A Few Figs ...,* a collection of saucy, defiant poems, established her as "the voice of rebellious youth" and "spokesman for the new woman." It was a great popular success.

When Edna went to Paris, in 1921, to write articles for *Vanity Fair,* she met the Benéts, Edgar Lee Masters, and F. Scott Fitzgerald. She wrote some poetry as well as her "Nancy Boyd" pieces, and traveled about Europe.

The Harp-Weaver..., published upon her return, won the Pulitzer Prize. It included some of her finest sonnets. That year (1923) she met and married Eugen Boissevain, a Dutch importer and a widower, whose wife, Inez Milholland, had been a suffrage leader. They traveled around the world, then settled at "Steepletop," a farm near Austerlitz, N.Y. Boissevain directed the household; Edna wrote — poems and the libretto for Deems Taylor's opera *The King's Henchman*, performed at the Metropolitan to great acclaim: said one reviewer — "the best American opera we have ever heard."

A confirmed feminist since college, Millay read her poetry at a dedication ceremony of the National Woman's Party in Washington, D.C., in 1923. And, in 1927 in Boston, she marched — and read her poem "Justice Denied In Massachusetts" — to protest the verdict to execute Sacco and Vanzetti.

The poetry of Millay's middle years is less brash and defiant, more reflective, but still personal, lyric. She rejected T.S. Eliot and the new criticism, and there was little critical praise for *The Buck in the Snow* and *Wine from These Grapes.* Her later works, focusing on social and political issues, are more propaganda than poetry — and Millay knew it: they were written in haste for a cause. Since the 1960s critics have condemned her less for ignoring the new poetry, recognizing the enduring merit of the lyrical poems she cast in traditional forms.

BY CHARLES ELLIS

1892 Born Feb. 22 Rockland, Me.

1917 Graduated from Vassar College

1917 Published *Renascence*

1920 Published *A Few Figs from Thistles*

1921-23 Staff writer, *Vanity Fair*

1923 Published *Ballad of the Harp-Weaver*

1923 Married Eugen Jan Boissevain

1927 Wrote *The King's Henchman* (opera)

1928 Published *The Buck in the Snow*

1931 Published *Fatal Interview*

1934 Published *Wine from These Grapes*

1937 Published *Conversations at Midnight*

1939 Published *Huntsman, What Quarry?*

1940 Published *Make Bright the Arrows*

1940 Elected to American Academy of Arts & Letters

1950 Died Oct 19 Austerlitz, N.Y.

MARIA MITCHELL

America's first woman astronomer, Maria Mitchell was a distinguished scientist who discovered a new comet, a brilliant teacher who inspired the first generation of Vassar students and helped establish a standard of excellence at that college. She was the first woman elected to the American Academy of Arts & Sciences.

As a child Maria revealed insatiable curiosity and exceptional powers of observation — traits that her father, an amateur astronomer, shared and appreciated. She assisted him with calculations and celestial observations from the widow's walk on their house in Nantucket, then the world's greatest whaling port, where knowledge of the stars had special value. She studied under Cyrus Peirce, later head of the first normal school, who instilled a passion for accuracy.

A job as a librarian of the Nantucket Athenaeum gave Mitchell the opportunity — and the resources — to pursue her study of mathematics and navigation at her own pace. She mastered Bridge's *Conic Sections*, Hutton's *Mathematics*, Bowditch's *Practical Navigation*; she read the works of Lagrange and Laplace in French. A small "observatory" built atop their house afforded Maria and her father a place to use new instruments, like the four-inch telescope provided by the U.S. Coast Survey, for which they made official observations. William Bond, director of the Harvard Observatory, and Alexander Bache of the Coast Survey assisted and advised them, recognizing the dedication, knowledge and ability of father and daughter.

On the night of October 1, 1847, Maria discovered a new comet, which was named after her — and for which the King of Denmark awarded her a gold medal. Other honors followed: recognition by the American Association for the Advancement of Science, the Smithsonian Institution, and the American Academy of Arts and Sciences. And she was appointed to provide astronomical calculations for the *Nautical Almanac*. Her fame preceded her to Europe, where, in 1857, she visited Greenwich and other observatories, and met celebrated mathematician Mary Somerville, scientist Alexander von Humbolt, and Charles Babbage, inventor of the calculating machine.

On her return she was given a five-inch telescope by Elizabeth Peabody and other influential women in the name of "the women of America," an instrument permitting more precise observation. With it, in 1858, she discovered Donati's Comet independently.

An offer to become professor of astronomy at Matthew Vassar's new women's college, created to match the best men's colleges, surprised self-educated Maria Mitchell, but she accepted — and was the most celebrated member of the first faculty. Vassar provided an observatory with a twelve-inch telescope for Maria and her father. Independent, forthright Maria Mitchell became a demanding — quite unorthodox — teacher. She refused to grade students or record absences, but she taught students to observe and to think: "Question everything" was her refrain. Students helped in the observatory; some bought telescopes; many became scientists — twenty-five are listed in *Who's Who in America*.

Mitchell continued research. She pioneered in photographing sunspots, studied the surfaces of the planets. And she championed the use of scientific method on social problems. At Vassar she became a legend.

1818   Born Aug. 1 Nantucket, Mass.

1836-60   Librarian, Nantucket Athenaeum

1847   Discovered new comet

1848   Elected to American Academy of Arts & Sciences

1865-88   Professor of Astronomy, Vassar College

1869   Elected to American Philosophical Society

1873   Founded Association for Advancement of Women

1889   Died June, 28 Lynn, Mass.

FLANNERY O'CONNOR

Flannery O'Connor created powerful and startlingly original stories and novels. Struck at 25 with a crippling — and ultimately fatal — disease, she managed to write fiction that won critical acclaim and numerous awards, producing a body of work that places her in the first rank of 20th-century American writers.

Born into a Southern, Catholic family, Flannery O'Connor was fifteen when her father died, after prolonged illness, of lupus erythematosus, the illness that would later strike her. As a child she kept a journal, wrote poems and stories. At college she wrote for the literary magazine and was editor of her yearbook. While she was attending the Writer's Workshop at the University of Iowa, her first story was published in *Accent*. For a time she lived in New York and Connecticut: other stories appeared in *Mademoiselle, Sewanee Review, Partisan Review*. Then, in 1950, she had her first major attack of lupus; for the rest of her life she lived with her mother on a farm near Milledgeville, Georgia.

Wise Blood, her first novel, earned impressive reviews. Although the story of a deeply religious man who blinds himself as an act of atonement puzzled most critics, they recognized it as a tale of chilling power, expertly wrought with vividly rendered characters. The critic Caroline Gordon, who compared O'Connor to Kafka, observed: "Her picture of the modern world is literally terrifying."

Publication of a collection of short stories in 1955 brought Miss O'Connor wider recognition. Again, religious beliefs underlie the plots: in several stories disaster brings the protagonist to a kind of salvation. In spite of her illness, she lectured at several colleges and universities. She received grants from the National Institute of Arts and Letters and the Ford Foundation and, with dwindling strength, continued to write.

In her second novel, *The Violent Bear It Away*, the protagonist — a kind of prophet — contends with the depravities of the world in another story fraught with religious symbolism. The novel centers on his baptizing — and drowning — his idiot cousin, the kind of grotesque, violent action, used for a purpose, characteristic of O'Connor's work. Of the novelist's art, O'Connor observed: "The writer's gaze has to extend beyond the surface, beyond mere problems, until it touches the realm of mystery which is the concern of the prophets. True prophecy in the novelist's case is a matter of seeing near things with their extensions of meaning . . . ." Deformed characters, bizarre incidents, improbable comedy, stark tragedy, a Southern setting — all, suffused with a sense of mystery, are elements in the world of Flannery O'Connor's fiction.

Each new work, however challenging to readers, added to Miss O'Connor's reputation. Translations of her books were published in Europe and Japan. She was awarded honorary degrees by St. Mary's Collge at Notre Dame and Smith Collge. After her death, *The Complete Stories* . . . won the National Book Award.

1925	Born Mar. 25 Savannah, Ga.
1945	Graduate from Georgia State College
1946	Published "The Geranium" in *Accent*
1947	Graduated from University of Iowa (MFA)
1952	Published *Wise Blood*
1955	Published *A Good Man Is Hard To Find* (Short Stories)

1959	Published *The Violent Bear It Away*
1964	Died Aug. 3 Milledgeville, Ga.
1965	*Everything That Rised Must Converge* (Short Stories) published
1971	*The Complete Stories of Flannery O'Connor* published
1978	*Letters* published

ALICE PAUL

Founder of the National Woman's Party and the militant wing of the suffrage movement, Alice Paul devoted herself with awesome intensity to the twin
goals of women's suffrage and equal rights. For eight years before the Federal
suffrage amendment was ratified, she conceived and directed a campaign of
political activism of unprecedented scope and impact; for the next fifty years
she kept the issue of ERA alive. "I always thought," she observed, "once you
put your hand to the plough you don't remove it until you get to the end of
the row."

Raised in a Quaker home where equality was taken for granted, Alice Paul,
after graduating from college, plunged into social work in the slums of New
York and then London. In England she joined the suffragist forces of Emmeline
Pankhurst, whose suffagettes engaged in a kind of political guerrilla warfare,
using revolutionary methods to influence Parliament and the nation. For three
years Miss Paul worked with the Pankhursts: she demonstrated, was jailed three
times, went on hunger strikes and was force-fed. She had found her cause and
her method; she returned to America, in 1910, committed to both.

The National American Woman Suffrage Association had for years concentrated on winning suffrage State by State; by 1911 six Western States had en-
franchised women. Alice Paul saw this process as slow — and futile. She proposed to concentrate on the Federal amendment, to hold the Party in power
responsible, and to use the women's vote in the six suffrage States for political
leverage in Congress. The NAWSA appointed Miss Paul chairman of its dor-
mant Congressional Committee — with no financial support. Alice Paul and
two assistants undertook to raise funds and establish a beachhead in Washington.

With an intensity that either shocked or inspired volunteers, Alice Paul
recruited and organized a group that managed massive demonstrations like the
march of 5000 women down Washington's Pennsylvania Avenue the day before
President Woodrow Wilson's inauguration. Alice Paul led deputations to the
White House and to Congress. The women lobbied, marched, maintained a
picket line at the White House, burned the President's speeches in Lafayette
Square, built watch fires in front of the White House — and were frequently
arrested, sometimes treated brutally. Miss Paul and her followers — by 1916
a separate National Woman's Party — maintained constant ferment, keeping
the suffrage movement on the front pages of America's papers

In each step of the legislative process, as the suffrage amendment wove its
way through Congressional committees, Alice Paul and her lobbyists kept
pressure on committee members. Once the amendment was passed, the Woman's
Party brought political pressure on reluctant States, helping secure ratification.
Historians generally agree that Miss Paul's militancy complemented NAWSA's
more conservative approach, that each in its own way contributed to final
victory.

In 1923 Alice Paul helped draft the Equal Rights Amendment, and for the
rest of her life she labored for its passage — and for equal rights for women
world-wide.

1885	Born Jan. 11 Moorestown, N.J.	1916	Founded National Woman's Party
1905	Graduated from Swarthmore College	1922	Received LL B from American University
1907	Received MA from University of Pennsylvania		
1907-10	Student, social worker in England	1927	Received LL M from American University
1912	Received PhD from University of Pennsylvania	1928	Received DC L from American University
1912	Chairman, Congressional Committee, NAWSA	1939	Founded World Women's Party
1913	Formed Congressional Union	1977	Died Jul. 9 Moorestown, N.J.

FRANCES PERKINS

Through the first three decades of this century she worked with singular dedication to improve conditions for America's working men and women, and, in 1933, she became the U.S. Secretary of Labor, the first woman appointed to a U.S. Cabinet. Convinced early that legislation and firm enforcement could best remedy the ills of factories and sweatshops, Frances Perkins spent most of her life either lobbying for labor laws or administering agencies that enforced them.

At Mount Holyoke College, Frances Perkins gained a strong sense of mission and, through a course that included surveys of working conditions of local factories, a cause worthy of dedicated effort. In Chicago she taught school and spent her free time working at settlement houses (Hull House and Chicago Commons); she collected wages owed immigrants and learned first-hand about working conditions and unscrupulous employers.

Frances Perkins left teaching to undertake social work in Philadelphia, where she, single-handed, challenged dishonest employment agencies, courageously faced down a personal threat, and helped secure an ordinance requiring agency licensing. She moved to New York, studied sociology at Columbia, became a suffragist speaker, and, as secretary of the New York Consumers' League, worked for improved sanitary and safety conditions in bakeries and other shops and lobbied in Albany for a 54-hour workweek bill, which was passed with the help of State Senator Alfred E. Smith.

On March 25, 1911, Frances Perkins witnessed the fire at the Triangle Shirtwaist Co., which took 146 lives, and she became secretary of the Committee on Safety, a citizen's group formed after that tragedy. She worked with the State Factory Investigation Commission, inspecting factories throughout the State and preparing and supporting legislation. After her marriage — to economist Paul Wilson, she did volunteer work, but his investment losses and subsequent illness led her to accept Governor Alfred Smith's appintment to the N.Y. Industrial Commission, the first woman commissioner. She reorganized and revitalized the State's factory inspection system and assisted in settling a strike of 4400 workers in Rome, N.Y. Smith was defeated in 1920; when re-elected, he appointed her to the new Industrial Board

Under Governors Smith and Roosevelt, Frances Perkins led the effort to improve conditions for workers in New York State. She supported and administered the Workmen's Compensation Act, advocated protective legislation for women (instead of Alice Paul's ERA) and a child-labor law, and, in the Depression, worked for state unemployment insurance and emergency relief measures.

As President Roosevelt's Secretary of Labor, she played a leading role in developing some of the landmark legislation of the New Deal: the Civilian Conservation Corps Act, the National Labor Relations Act, the Social Security Act, and the National Industrial Recovery Act. Within her department she cleaned up a tainted Immigration Service, expanded the Bureau of Labor Statistics, and established a division of Labor Standards. The first Madam Secretary, a steadfast champion of social justice, proved one of the most effective members of the Roosevelt Cabinet.

1880	Born Apr.10 Boston, Mass.	1913	Married Paul Wilson
1902	Graduated from Mount Holyoke College	1919-21	Member, N.Y. State Industrial Commission
1904-7	Teacher, Ferry Hill School, Lake Forest, Ill.	1923-27	Member, N.Y. State Industrial Board
1907-9	Secretary, Philadelphia Research & Protective League	1928-33	Industrial Commissioner of N.Y.
1910	Received MA from Columbia U.	1933-46	U.S. Secretary of Labor
1910-12	Secretary, N.Y. Consumers' League	1945-53	Commissioner, U.S. Civil Service Commission
1912-15	Secretary, Committee on Safety of City of N.Y.	1957-65	Professor, Cornell University
		1965	Died May 14, New York, N.Y.

79

JEANNETTE RANKIN

Reformer, feminist, suffragist, pacifist, politician — Jeannette Rankin was the first woman elected to the U.S. House of Representatives, three years before passage of the 19th Amendment enfranchising women. Unalterably opposed to war, she was the only member of Congress to vote against U.S. entry into both world wars.

After college, Jeannette Rankin worked briefly as a teacher and social worker. While doing graduate study at the University of Washington she became involved in women suffrage efforts in that State. Success there led her to become a field worker for the National American Woman's Suffrage Association: she covered fifteen States and helped win the vote for women in her home State, Montana, in 1914. Two years later, the men and women of Montana elected her to the U.S. Congress, and on April 2, 1917, she became the first woman member of Congess.

"I want to stand by my country, but I cannot vote for war," Jeannette Rankin told Congress as she joined forty-nine other members in voting against U.S. entry into World War I. She originated legislation to aid women, worked for passage of the Federal suffrage amendment, and championed the cause of workers in industry and government. In 1918 she failed in an attempt to win nomination as a candidate for the U.S. Senate.

After leaving office Miss Rankin continued to work for the cause of women — and for peace. She went with Jane Addams to Zurich as a delegate to the Second International Congress of Women, then did field work for the National Consumers' League and the Women's International League for Peace and Freedom. She served as a lobbyist for the Women's Peace Union, which supported a constitutional amendment banning war, and after several years in a winter home in Georgia, she joined with faculty members of the University of Georgia in establishing the Georgia Peace Society. During the 1930s she represented the National Council for the Prevention of War — in Washington and in the field.

Running as an anti-war candidate, Jeannette Rankin was again elected to Congress in 1940. In Washington she took a stand against increased arms appropriations, the draft, Lend-Lease. On the day after Pearl Harbor, she was the only member of Congress to vote against the Declaration of War. She was not re-elected.

In private life Miss Rankin continued her work for peace. She became interested in the pacifist approach to politics in other countries and after the war visited India to study Ghandi's methods. In the next two decades she traveled extensively in Europe, Asia, Africa and South America. As the war in Vietnam was expanded under President Lyndon Johnson, she was persuaded to head the Jeannette Rankin Brigade: in January 1968, at 87, she led 5000 women in a peaceful march on the U.S. Capitol in Washington, protesting U.S. involvement in Southeast Asia. For over fifty years she had unswervingly pursued the ideal of peace: "You take people as far as they will go," she observed, "not as far as you would like them to go."

1880	Born Jun. 11 Missoula, Mont.	1919	Delegate, Second International Congress of Women
1902	Graduated from University of Montana	1920-24	Field Secretary, National Consumers' League
1908-09	Attended New York School of Philanthropy	1928	Founded Georgia Peace Society
1909-10	Attended University of Washington	1929-39	Field Organizer, National Council for Prevention of War
1911-12	Field worker, New York Woman Suffrage Party	1941-43	Member, U.S. Congress
1912-17	Field Secretary, National American Woman Suffrage Assoc.	1968	Led Jeannette Rankin Brigade peace march, Washington, D.C.
1917-19	Member, U.S. Congress	1973	Died May 18 Carmel, Calif.

ELEANOR ROOSEVELT

Like Abigail Adams, Eleanor Roosevelt transcended her role as wife of a President of the United States and, in a far more public life, devoted herself to causes of humanity with a spirit, grace and tenacity that ultimately won her an unprecedented place as "First Lady of the World."

Orphaned at nine, Eleanor Roosevelt was raised by her grandmother. At the Allenswood School in England, she was influenced by the headmistress, Marie Souvestre, who embraced unpopular causes. Afterwards, in New York, eighteen-year-old Eleanor taught at a settlement house and, as a member of the National Consumers' League, visited factories and sweatshops to investigate the health and safety of workers. She was involved in social work when she became engaged to her fifth cousin Franklin; her "Uncle Ted," the President, attended the wedding.

Almost from the start the marriage was marred by the presence — and the personality — of Franklin's mother, who at times lived with them and dominated their household. Raising her family occupied Eleanor until her husband entered politics. In Washington, when Franklin was Assistant Secretary of the Navy, she dutifully performed her social functions, but turned to Red Cross activities during World War I. After Franklin was stricken with infantile paralysis in 1921, she became more active in social service and, for his sake, in State political affairs.

Eleanor Roosevelt proved an effective political organizer; in 1924 she mobilized women through New York State to support the Democratic Party and led a delegation to the Democratic National Convention. In 1928, when Franklin was elected governor, she directed the national women's campaign for the party. By 1932, when she coordinated activities of the Women's Division of the party, she had become a leading women's activist.

In the White House Eleanor Roosevelt expanded on this role: she helped secure appointments in Government for women and became the center of a network of women devoted to the causes of women and of social welfare, an unofficial yet effective channel to the sources of power in Government. With the President's mobility limited, Mrs. Roosevelt traveled extensively throughout the country, visiting coal mines, slum areas and relief projects, speaking out for the disadvantaged. Through her newspaper column, "My Day," and radio talks, she reached millions. Her advocacy of the poor brought her thousands of letters (over 300,000 in 1933) — appeals for help which she answered personally (100 a day) or sent to Government agencies for action. During the war she visited military camps and hospitals in the U.S. and overseas.

After Franklin Roosevelt's death, President Truman appointed Mrs. Roosevelt a delegate to the United Nations, where she won world acclaim for her forceful sponsorship of the UN's Declaration of Human Rights, perhaps her crowning achievement. Throughout her extremely active life she tirelessly championed the underprivileged, minorities, the poor — in America and throughout the world. At her memorial service, Adlai Stevenson asked, "What other single human being has touched and transformed the existence of so many?"

BY DANIEL GREENE · FRANKLIN D. ROOSEVELT LIBRARY

1884 Born Oct. 11 New York, N.Y.

1899-1902 Attended Allenswood School, England

1905 Married Franklin Roosevelt

1921- Board member, League of Women Voters

1927-33 Vice-President, Todhunter School, New York, N.Y.

1933 Published *It's Up to the Women*

1936 Published *My Day*

1937 Published *This Is My Story*

1940 Published *The Moral Basis of Democracy*

1945 Delegate, U.N. General Assembly

1946-53 Chairman, U.N. Commission on Human Rights

1949 Published *This I Remember*

1958 Published *On My Own*

1961-62 Chairman, Presidential Commission on Status of Women

1962 Died Nov. 7 New York, N.Y.

MARGARET SANGER

The leading crusader in America for birth control (a term she coined), Margaret Sanger was arrested eight times in a tumultuous career that brought her condemnations as a "lascivious monster" and praise — by H.G. Wells — as the "the greatest woman in the world." She opened the first birth-control clinic in America, the first clinic staffed by doctors, and led the national movement which became the Planned Parenthood Federation.

The sixth of eleven children of Anne and Michael Higgins, an improvident stonemason, Margaret Higgins witnessed her mother, prematurely aged by bearing and rearing children, work herself to an early death. Margaret's sisters paid her college tuition; she left college to try teaching, then studied nursing. Architect William Sanger, an idealist like her father, persuaded Margaret to elope; they had three children. After ten years of marriage, she began to work as a nurse in New York City: she lectured on health to young mothers and wrote articles for the left-wing *The Call*. Her column "What Every Girl Should Know", designed to introduce adolescents to the subject of sex, was suppressed by the Post Office Department, then vigorously enforcing the Comstock Act of 1873, whose sweeping provisions prohibited distribution of information on sex even for medical purposes.

As Margaret Sanger worked as a nurse and midwife in New York tenements, she learned first-hand of the suffering and death of women resulting from ignorance, venereal disease and crude abortions. The death of Sadie Sachs, the wife of a truck driver, which she witnessed, profoundly affected her; it was a turning point — Margaret Sanger had a cause.

She traveled to Europe to gain information, and returned to start a magazine, *The Woman Rebel*, which championed women's freedoms, particularly a woman's right to determine her maternity. The Post Office again acted: she was indicted — and fled to Europe, but copies of her pamphlet *Family Limitations*, describing French birth-control methods, were distributed. In Holland Margaret Sanger learned of the free birth-control clinic established by Aletta Jacobs, first female Dutch physician, which offered contraceptive counsel for the first time in history, and she underwent training in the Dutch system.

Mrs. Sanger returned to a more sympathetic America. Her husband had been jailed, through entrappement, for handing out one copy of *Family Limitations*; then her daughter died of pneumonia — a story covered by the press. Influential New York women and writers offered support; the Government finally dropped its case. After a lecture tour, she opened the first birth-control clinic in America in Brooklyn, for which she was arrested.

In New York in 1921 Margaret Sanger organized the first National Birth Control Conference, and hundreds of doctors attended the educational sessions. Two years later she opened the first doctor-staffed clinic, which maintained clinical records and provided physicians instruction; it served as a model for over 300 clinics later opened through the U.S. In 1937, when the Comstock Act was reversed, Margaret Sanger was already concentrating on the world movement.

1879	Born Sep. 14 Corning, N.Y.	1920	Published *Women and the New Race*
1893-96	Attended Claverack College	1921	Founded the American Birth Control League
1900-02	Attended Nursing School, White Plains (N.Y.) Hospital	1922	Married J. Noah Slee
1902	Married William Sanger; divorced 1920	1923	Established Birth Control Clinical Research Bureau
1916	Opened first American birth-control clinic	1926	Published *Happiness in Marriage*
		1966	Died Sep. 6 Tucson, Ariz.

ELIZABETH BAYLEY SETON

A convert to Catholicism, Elizabeth Bayley Seton founded the American Sisters of Charity, the first religious community of women in the United States. She was canonized in 1975 — America's first saint.

Elizabeth Bayley was three years old when her mother died; she was raised by her father's relatives and by her stepmother, a devout Episcopalian. At a private school Elizabeth mastered French and the piano. She was married, at 19, to William Seton, a successful merchant; they had five children. Mrs. Seton undertook charitable work, and in 1797 founded a society to aid widowed mothers, the first charitable organization in New York. After her husband's business, then his health, failed, they went to Italy. Her husband's death left her with his business associates, Antonio and Filippo Filicchi, who introduced her to the teachings of the Roman Catholic Church. Deeply religious from childhood, Elizabeth Seton spent a tortured year of soul searching: in March 1805 she became a Catholic.

After her conversion, friends — and even her godmother — deserted her. An attempt to start a school in New York City failed, and for a time she operated a boarding house. Stirred to serve God and the poor, she considered joining a convent in Canada; instead, she accepted the invitation of the president of St. Mary's College in Baltimore to start a school for girls there.

Part of the land granted the Catholic Cecil Calvert (Lord Baltimore), Baltimore was the first Catholic See in America — in 1808 more hospitable to Catholics than New York. By December 1808 Mrs. Seton had ten girls in her school, which was located next to St. Mary's College. Her program included religious instruction, and, at the request of Archbishop John Carroll, she prepared children for their first communion. She established religious routines at the school and began to consider starting a religious community. Impressed by her exemplary piety, members of the clergy encouraged her, and on December 7, 1808, the first candidate joined her; in March 1809 Mrs. Seton took her vows.

In June Mother Seton and the first members of her community moved to Emmitsburg, Maryland. By fall, sixteen people occupied a four-room farmhouse. Conditions were primitive: water was carried from a spring; snow sifted into the sleeping rooms. In 1810 the growing community moved to a larger building, St. Joseph's House. The sisters cared for the sick and the poor and conducted a small boarding school for girls (St. Joseph's). Girls of the local parish received free schooling — the beginnings of parish schools. A copy of the rule of the Sisters of Charity of St. Vincent de Paul was brought from France; in modified form it became the rule of the new order.

Within a year the school had forty students. Mother Seton proved an effective teacher and manager — a gentle, pious leader. The order spread to Philadelphia, to New York, ultimately across the nation, establishing schools, orphanages and hospitals, a powerful — and enduring — force for good in America.

ARCHIVES, ST. JOSEPH'S PROVINCIAL HOUSE

1774	Born Aug. 28 New York, N.Y.
1794	Married William Seton; died 1803
1797	Founded Society for Relief of Poor Widows
1803-04	Visited Italy
1808	Founded girls' school (later St. Joseph's)
1809	Founded Sisters of Charity of St. Joseph
1810	Founded parish school
1821	Died Jan. 4 Emmitsburg, Md.

BESSIE SMITH

"The Queen of the Blues," "One of the greatest performers America produced" — Bessie Smith won stardom as America's premiere blues singer in the 1920's, reaching millions through performances in vaudeville and on records and radio. A performer of extraordinary power with unmatched vocal abilities, she broke attendance records at the theatres throughout the country and created records with phenomenal sales, such as "Down Hearted Blues," with over 700,000 sold in six months.

Bessie and her brother Clarence, a dancer, joined a road show playing in Chattanooga in 1912; the next year she was singing at the "81" Theatre in Atlanta — such a natural singer that, after her performances, people threw money on the stage. For several years she traveled the black vaudeville circuit and by 1920 was appearing as a single, occasionally with her own show.

Among the first records Bessie Smith made for Columbia Phonograph Co. in 1923 was "Down Hearted Blues"; its sensational sales made her, almost overnight, "the famous Columbia recording artist." A triumphant return to the "81" in Atlanta — as the star — was broadcast over radio. At the Frolic Theatre in Birmingham, streets were blocked by the overflow crowds; at the Koppin Theatre in Detroit Bessie's opening caused a near riot; it was the same in city after city. That year Bessie married Jack Gee, who helped manage her shows.

By 1925 Bessie was writing her own lyrics — "Sorrowful Blues" and "Rocking Chair Blues" — and performing with top accompanists. Jazz history was made on January 14, 1925, when Bessie and Louis Armstrong made what many critics consider the definitive records of W.C. Handy's "St. Louis Blues." Her life had fallen into a pattern: a series of triumphant road shows — "tent" shows in summer — punctuated by recording sessions in New York. Her company traveled in a custom-made, yellow railroad car; she continued to make hit records like "Money Blues"; in 1926 her career reached its zenith.

Bessie wrote her most famous song, "Black Water Blues," in 1927 and recorded it with James Johnson, her finest piano accompaniest. One summer night that year, Bessie, alone, chased away hooded KKK Klansmen gathered outside the show tent. "Poor Man's Blues," which Bessie wrote and recorded in 1928, is a song of social protest some consider her finest record. The next year she starred in one of the early talking pictures, *St. Louis Blues*, her only film.

The record market collapsed in the early 1930's, and Bessie's road show struggled through the Depression years until in 1937, when she was about to make more records and another film, she was fatally injured in an automobile accident.

Millions had heard Bessie's rich, powerful contralto, captured on 160 records; some knew also of her wild, sometimes violent tears, her earthiness, her impulsive generosity. Bessie Smith was an original: she sang — and lived — intensely. "She had music in her soul," Louis Armstrong observed. And Mahlia Jackson: "Her music haunted you even when she stopped singing."

1894 Born Apr. 15 Chattanooga, Tenn.

1912- Vaudeville singer

1923-31 Recording artist, Columbia
  Phonograph Co.

1923 Married Jack Gee

1923- Starred in road shows

1929 Starred in film, *St. Louis Blues*

1930 Starred in *Happy Times*

1937 Died Sep. 26 Clarksville, Miss.

ELIZABETH CADY STANTON

Elizabeth Cady Stanton organized the first women's rights convention in America — in Seneca Falls, N.Y. — and there for the first time publicly demanded the vote for women. She and Susan Anthony became the prime movers of the women's movement, building a national organization dedicated to obtaining women's suffrage.

When Elizabeth Cady was ten, her only brother died, and her father cried: "Oh, my daughter, I wish you were a boy!" In her autobiography Cady Stanton revealed that she then resolved to be as self-reliant and independent as any boy.

After Elizabeth Cady married Henry Stanton, an abolitionist, the Stantons went to London, where Mr. Stanton attended the World's Anti-Slavery Convention. There the policy of excluding women delegates enraged Mrs. Stanton, as well as Lucretia Mott, a delegate from Philadelphia; the two decided to organize a women's rights convention in the United States. The Stantons settled in Seneca Falls, N.Y. and Mrs. Stanton began a personal campaign to improve women's plight. In July 1848, when Lucretia Mott visited the area, the two were ready to carry out their plan.

The convention held on July 19-20 attracted over 300 people to Seneca Falls; Cady Stanton presented a list of eighteen grievances modeled after the Declaration of Independence and then added a resolution demanding suffrage for women. Most newspapers ridiculed the convention. Cady Stanton began writing articles, some published in Amelia Bloomer's newspaper *Lily*. Through Mrs. Bloomer she met Susan Anthony, and the two were soon working together: "Night after night by an old-fashioned fireplace," Stanton later wrote, "we plotted and planned the coming agitation."

While Anthony campaigned, Stanton wrote articles, as well as speeches for both. In 1854 she addressed a committee of the N.Y. senate, in 1860 both houses — and achieved passage of an improved property law. She startled several conventions with her proposals for liberalized divorce laws. Unlike Anthony, she was always the champion of the mistreated housewife. As co-editor of the feminist *Revolution*, she attacked all forms of discrimination against women; after the paper failed, she and Anthony agreed to focus on suffrage: they founded the National Woman's Suffrage Association.

Mrs. Stanton took the cause of feminism on the Lyceum circuit: for a dozen years she traveled extensively giving lectures. Her animated style, wit and graciousness won her — if not always her cause — a wide following. Her pen was also busy: she wrote the Women's Declaration of Rights for the Centennial Exposition (1876), the multi-volume *History of Woman Suffrage* (with Anthony), and her autobiography.

Although Stanton shared Anthony's devotion to the cause of women's suffrage, she strove, in addition, to liberate women from "religious and social bondage" as well. More radical than Anthony, she was the 19th century's most celebrated advocate of complete equality for women.

NATIONAL WOMAN'S PARTY

1815	Born Nov. 12 Johnstown, N.Y.
1832	Graduated from Troy Female Seminary
1840	Married Henry Stanton
1848	Organized Women's Rights Convention
1952	Founded N.Y. State Women's Temperance Society
1868	Founded Working Women's Association (with Anthony)
1869	Founded National Woman Suffrage Association (with Anthony)
1881	Published first volume of *History of Woman Suffrage*
1890-92	President, National American Woman Suffrage Association
1895	Published *Woman's Bible*
1898	Published *Eighty Years and More*
1902	Died Nov. 12 New York, N.Y.

GERTRUDE STEIN

In the first decades of the 20th century Gertrude Stein daringly brought the new theories of cubism and abstract painting to the art of writing, working with ideas of Braque, Picasso, Matisse and others to produce writings that pushed language near — and often beyond — the limits of the intelligible. As an early champion of abstract painting, she also reigned over one of the most celebrated salons in Paris.

As a child Gertrude read widely. At Harvard Annex she studied psychology under William James and co-authored a study which concluded that individuals reveal their essential character through repetitions of speech and other patterns of behavior.

In 1903 she went to Paris. She began a novel, translated — and copied — Flaubert, and plunged into the art world of the Left Bank. Unframed paintings by Monet, Cezanne, Matisse, Renoir and others covered the walls of her *pavillon*. The new techniques of these painters — bold strokes and colors and absence of detail — influenced her writing. Her mulatto girl in *Three Lives* has no past and no definite physical features. This was the first step. Then she met Picasso.

Picasso's emphasis on the "now" led Stein to try to capture the present in words and to experiment with the idea that people reveal themselves through repetitions and slight variations of speech patterns. In her "portrait" of Picasso, she wrote: "This one was one having always something being coming out of him, something have completely a real meaning. This one was one who was working and he was one needing this thing needing to be working...." She was trying to create meaning by applying language in layers like daubs of color.

Stein was encouraged in her work by Alice Toklas, whom she met in Paris. They became inseparable: Alice became housekeeper, typist, confidante.

Under Picasso's continuing influence, Stein journeyed further into the incomprehensible; his cubist still lifes and collages with snippets of cloth, paper, etc. led Stein, in turn, to break up her sentences and scramble the fragments. A collection of such experiments was published as *Tender Buttons*, a book that attracted critical attention but little praise.

After World War I Stein's salon became a literary mecca: Hemingway, Sherwood Anderson, F. Scott Fitzgerald and Ezra Pound were regulars. Stein's influence was greatest on Hemingway: he adopted — and modified — some of her techniques and, in turn, arranged publication of *The Making of Americans*, which added to her reputation as an innovative writer. But it was her tongue-in-cheek *Autobiography of Alice B. Toklas* that brought Stein wide recognition. She collaborated with composer Virgil Thompson on an opera which won praise in America, and, in 1934, she returned triumphantly to the U.S..

Never easy reading, Stein's writings yet influenced an entire school of American writers. Although some — including Braque and Matisse — thought her grasp of painting superficial, she played a prominent role in the development of modern painting. In the arts she was one of the most influential women in the first half of the 20th century.

BY PABLO PICASSO   METROPOLITAN MUSEUM OF ART

1874	Born Feb. 3 Allegheny, Penn.
1897- 1902	Attended Johns Hopkins Medical School University
1898	Graduated from Radcliffe College
1909	Published *Three Lives*
1914	Published *Tender Buttons*

1925	Published *The Making of Americans*
1933	Published *Autobiography of Alice B. Toklas*
1937	Published *Everyone's Autobiography*
1945	Published *Wars I Have Seen*
1946	Died July. 27 Meuilly-sur-Seine, France

LUCY STONE

Shocked at her mother's inferior role in the family, Lucy Stone vowed early to remedy that situation and never to marry. She became a founder of the women's movement, but, at 37, she decided to marry: she was, however, the first woman in America to use her own name after marriage, giving her name to the practice.

As a child, Lucy questioned the Biblical authority for male dominance; she resolved to go to college to study Greek and Hebrew, to read the original. She taught school to earn money to attend college, where she learned enough Hebrew and Greek to detect mistranslations of the biblical passages concerning women.

An ardent abolitionist, Stone became a lecturer for the American Anti-slavery Society; a natural orator, she courageously faced ridicule and abuse. Gradually she added lectures on women's rights: "I was, " she stated, "a woman before I was an abolitionist. I must speak for women."

By 1850 Lucy Stone had dedicated herself to the women's movement. She led the call for the first national women's rights convention, held in Worcester, Massachusetts. Her speech there converted Susan B. Anthony to the cause. "Lucy Stone was the first speaker who really stirred the nation's heart on the subject of women's wrongs," Cady Stanton later wrote. For many lectures Lucy dared appear in bloomers, then a symbol of reform and liberation.

Henry Blackwell, a merchant and abolitionist, proposed to Lucy, offering marriage with complete freedom to continue her work. After much agonizing, Lucy accepted. At the ceremony Henry read a protest against the marriage laws. The name "Lucy Stone Blackwell" appeared in announcements, etc. for over a year; then, in July 1856, she wrote Susan Anthony to list her as "...Lucy Stone *only*...Leave off the Blackwell."

Lucy continued to travel and lecture. When her only child was born, in 1857, Lucy retired temporarily. In 1867 she resumed lecturing and in 1869 led the group that split with the Anthony wing of the movement. Both policies and personalities were involved: Stone sought women's suffrage through the States, Anthony through a Federal amendment; Stone supported a Federal Negro suffrage amendment — and tried to include women's suffrage; Anthony refused to support the amendment *unless* it included women's suffrage. Anthony and Stanton formed the National Woman's Suffrage Association, Stone the American Woman's Suffrage Association.

Stone helped found and edit the *Woman's Journal*, which carried the banner of the women's movement, but she did not support the labor movement, condemning strikes as "riotous proceedings." In this as in the suffrage struggle, she relied on the political system to right wrongs

When the two suffrage groups finally merged, in 1890, Lucy Stone became chairman of the executive committee. At the Columbian Exposition in Chicago in 1893, in one of her last speeches, she said, "I think, with never-ending gratitude, that the young women of today do not and can never know at what price their right to free speech and to speak at all in public has been earned." No one knew better.

1818 Born Aug. 13 W. Brookfield, Mass.	1855 Married Henry Blackwell
1847 Graduated from Oberlin College (First Massachusetts woman to receive college degree)	1869 Founded American Woman's Suffrage Association
1850 Organized Women's Rights Convention, Worcester, Mass.	1872-93 Founder, Editor, *Woman's Journal*
	1893 Died Oct. 18 Dorchester, Mass.

HARRIET BEECHER STOWE

"So this is the little lady who made this big war?" Abraham Lincoln said to the author of *Uncle Tom's Cabin* when she visited the White House in 1862. Her novel, graphically depicting the plight of slaves — the first to present blacks sympathetically — roused the conscience of the nation: it was one of the most influential novels in history.

Harriet Beecher was born into a family of ministers and reformers. Her father, Lyman, was a prominent Congregational revivalist; seven brothers were also ministers, the most famous, Henry Ward Beecher, a celebrated orator. Her elder sister Catherine was a stern, visionary educator.

Harriet attended Catherine's school in Hartford and later taught there — and at her school in Cincinnati. Harriet's first published work was a geography; then a sketch — her first fiction — won a magazine contest. In Cincinnati, with a slave State across the river, Harriet began to learn about slavery: she visited a Kentucky plantation and, from her own home, helped plan the escape of a black maid who was a fugitive slave.

At 24, shy, plain Harriet Beecher married the widowed Calvin Stowe, 33, professor of Bibical studies at her father's seminary in Cincinnati. In fifteen years she bore seven children, writing when she could. Publication of a collection of her stories convinced the family of her literary talent. "If I could use a pen as you can," her sister-in-law wrote, "I would write something that will make this whole nation feel what an accursed thing slavery is."

In 1850 the Stowes moved to Brunswick, Maine. Inspired at church one Sunday, Harriet returned home and wrote feverishly until she ran out of paper. She worked on her story for over a year, during which installments appeared in the *National Era*, an antislavery periodical published in Washington. The book, published in March 1852 in two volumes, was an immediate sensation — 3,000 copies sold the first day, 300,000 the first year. Publication of the novel could not have been more timely; passage of the Fugitive Slave Act in 1950 had sharpened Northern resistance to slavery: *Uncle Tom's Cabin* put the problem in moving human dimensions, with strong religious overtones. As never before, readers *felt* the evil of slavery. Harriet Beecher Stowe was feted in the North, damned in the South. A trip to England became a triumphant tour.

Her second antislavery novel, *Dred*, was far less successful, although it sold well. Her shorter pieces — some on slavery — were published in the *Alantic Monthly* and the *Christian Union*. For over twenty years she produced at least a book a year, most novels based on her childhood experiences in New England. *Poganuc People* comes the closest to autobiography.

Both Stowes were poor managers, and Harriet had to keep writing to support them. The later novels, hastily written to cover advances from publishers, are loosely constructed, undistinguished works, with some of the moral fervor but neither the relevance nor the timing that made *Uncle Tom's Cabin* a novel of unprecedented social and political consequence.

1811 Born Jun. 14 Litchfield, Conn.	1852 Published *Uncle Tom's Cabin*
1824-27 Attended Hartford Female Seminary	1856 Published *Dred*
1827-32 Teacher, Hartford Female Seminary	1862 Published *The Pearl of Orr's Island*
1832-36 Teacher, Western Female Seminary	1869 Published *Oldtown Folks*
1836 Married Calvin Stowe	1878 Published *Poganuc People*
1843 Published *The Mayflower* (Collection of stories)	1896 Died Jul. 1 Hartford, Conn.

MARTHA CAREY THOMAS

She championed excellence in higher education for women and, as first dean and then president of Bryn Mawr College, helped create an institution that from the beginning was of the first rank among American colleges. The high standards of scholarship Martha Carey Thomas resolutely maintained throughout her thirty-seven years as a college administrator ultimately influenced the quality of education for women — and men — in secondary schools, as well as colleges and universities, throughout America.

Seven-year-old Martha Thomas was almost fatally burned in a kitchen fire; during her extended convalescence she developed a love of reading. At school she demonstrated an inquisitive, retentive mind. Miss Slocum, a teacher at Howland Institute, told Martha she had the power of mind to be a great scholar. Resolved to pursue a life of study, Martha overcame her father's opposition and attended Cornell, where she continued to excel. At all-male Johns Hopkins University she was privately tutored in Greek but could not attend classes or earn a degree. Her search for quality education took her to Europe: at the University of Leipzig she was free to attend classes but had to go to the University of Zurich to obtain her degree — the first woman awarded a PhD *summa cum laude*. Her accomplishment brought some acclaim — in Europe and America.

Carey Thomas returned to America in time to offer her services — as president — to the new women's college planned for Bryn Mawr, Pennsylvania. Trustees selected an experienced man — James Rhoads, but named her dean and professor of English. Largely responsible for the curriculum and academic standards, Carey Thomas studied the programs of Smith, Wellesley, Vassar, Harvard Annex (later Radcliffe) and Harvard, and devised a program that combined a stiff entrance examination and rigorous academic standards with a liberal arts curriculum, an exceptional faculty, and well-stocked laboratories and library. Sensitive to charges that women's education was superficial, Dean Thomas held fast to high standards, and within a few years the college was recognized for its academic excellence.

When James Rhoads retired, Carey Thomas became president — as well as dean and later a trustee. With such large powers she directed all phases of operation — with firmness and vigor. She jealously watched standards, managed an extensive building program, brought distinguished guests to the campus (William Butler Yeats, Henry James), and strove — not always with success — to maintain an excellent faculty. Among her innovations was the creation of a department of education and a model school for teachers which incorporated the principles of John Dewey. A stimulating speaker, she was an effective spokeswoman for Bryn Mawr and for women's education.

A friend of Susan B. Anthony's, Carey Thomas became active in suffrage work — as speaker, fund-raiser and leader. As president, she made the National College Equal Suffrage League a rallying point among college women and an effective force within the national movement. With superlative Academic credentials and a distinguished career, Carey Thomas was a compelling advocate for women's education and suffrage.

1857   Born Jan. 2 Baltimore, Md.

1873-75   Attended Howland Institute

1877   Graduated from Cornell University

1877-78   Attended John Hopkins University

1879-82   Attended Leipzig University

1882   Received PhD from University of Zurich

1885   Helped found Bryn Mawr School for Girls

1885-1908   Dean, Bryn Mawr College

1894-22   President, Bryn Mawr College

1908   President, National College Women's Equal Suffrage League

1935   Died Dec. 2 Philadelphia, Penn.

IDA WELLS–BARNETT

With heroic courage she fought for equality for her race — in employment, at the polls, and before the law. Ida Wells–Barnett dared to tell the nation — and the world — the explicit horrors of lynchings and other practices by which prejudice, embodied in state law and custom, bent or evaded the intent of the 14th and 15th Amendments to the U.S. Constitution.

Young (21) Ida Wells was one of the first persons to sue a railroad for discrimination — after she had been forcibly removed from a coach. She won, but the decision was reversed by the State supreme court. Ida taught in Memphis schools and began writing articles for newspapers. While continuing to teach, she became editor and part owner of a small weekly, *Free Speech*. An article of hers protesting the inadequate schools available to Negro children led the Memphis school board to dismiss her, and she became a full-time journalist.

On March 9, 1892, three Negro men were lynched in Memphis. Ida Wells knew that the men's "crime" was competing successfully with white shopkeepers — and she spelled it out in her paper, denouncing the community for condoning lynchings. This proved a turning point in her life. She researched facts about other lynchings and published them. While she was visiting in New York, a mob destroyed her office.

As a writer for *New York Age*, Miss Wells continued her crusade against lynching. Articulate and poised, she became an effective speaker; she lectured in the Northeast, established some of the first Negro women's clubs and anti-lynching societies, and then carried her crusade to Great Britain, where she won strong support and founded an anti-lynching committee. In her effort to marshall world opinon, she published *A Red Record*, a statistical account of lynchings in the U.S. — which had tripled in a decade.

Miss Wells lectured extensively in the U.S. and settled in Chicago. She married Ferdinand Barnett, a lawyer and editor, and raised four children, but continued her work. As women's club president, she initiated social projects: the Negro Fellowship League, which she founded, was one of the first Negro settlement houses. Recognized as a fearless reporter who sought the facts, she went alone to the scene of lynchings and riots in Illinois and other States; her factual reports, published in newspapers and pamphlets, provided indisputable evidence of injustice and persecution to the public and helped save innocent lives.

Mrs. Wells–Barnett was one of the founders of the National Association for the Advancement of Colored People. She appreciated the value of suffrage (she wrote "How Enfranchisement Stops Lynching") and she founded the first Negro woman suffrage organization. Always the activist, she marched with the national suffrage organization in the parade in Washington the day before President Wilson's inauguration, and, as a member of the Equal Rights League, protested to President Wilson about segretation in Federal agencies. Her capacity for outrage remained undiminished.

1862	Born Jul. 16 Holly Springs, Miss.
1870-76	Studied at Rust University
1877-84	Teacher, Holly Springs schools
1884-91	Teacher, Memphis schools
1889-92	Editor, *Memphis Free Speech*
1892	Writer, *New York Age*
1893-94	Lectured in England, Scotland
1895	Married Ferdinand Barnett

1895	Published *A Red Record*
1910	Helped found NAACP
1910	Founded Negro Fellowship League
1913-16	Probation officer, Chicago municipal court
1914	Founded first Negro woman suffrage organization
1931	Died Mar. 25 Chicago, Ill.

EDITH WHARTON

Born to wealth, Edith Wharton wrote, with great authenticity, novels which depict the old New York aristocracy of the late 19th and early 20th centuries. Although not published until she was forty, she established herself as a novelist who could satisfy a large number of readers and yet win critical acclaim. In her lifetime, she wrote over fifty books, and the novels *Ethan Frome* and *The Age of Innocence* have secured a lasting place in American literature.

Edith Wharton's parents were from families who had long been part of New York society, and Edith grew up in a world which viewed artists and writers as Bohemians. Somehow, without renouncing wealth, Edith was yet able to rise above the privileged position of idle luxury to which she was born and devote herself to a life of writing.

Edith was taught by private tutors - at home and in Europe. By sixteen she had written and privately published a volume of poetry, but after her debut at seventeen, her life was, for almost a decade, dominated by her social world: fashionable parties and dances, courtship, a broken engagement, a somewhat sudden — and unhappy — marriage, and the idle life of New York, Newport and Europe.

In the 1890s she began to write. Two volumes of short stories appeared before the novel *The Valley of Decision*. Then came the first novel of manners, *The House of Mirth*, in which the rigid society of fashionable New York crushes a sensitive, nonconforming woman. Edith Wharton was never crushed by fashionable society, but its excesses and trivialities continued to haunt her. That society plays a prominent role in the *Custom of the Country* and *The Age of Innocence*, which won the Pulitzer Prize. In the former, Wharton satirizes the crude pursuit of social advancement; in the latter, she presents scenes of the society of her youth with memorable richness, in contrast to vapid, unfulfilled characters.

In her best-known novel — *Ethan Frome* — Wharton turned to the simple life of a New England town and the story of a doomed man caught in a fateful triangle. This powerful novel, frequently used in schools, is considered by many her finest work.

Some critics speculate that Edith's marriage to Teddy Wharton caused her to seek refuge in writing fiction. Edith's brilliance was too much for Teddy, who was happiest with horses and dogs. The couple traveled to Europe regularly, where Edith sought out men of intellect and culture like novelists Percy Lubbock and Henry James. After her divorce Edith spent more time in Europe.

Henry James and Edith became close friends, but only a few of her works reflect James' influence. Wharton's sharp eye and pen place her, as a novelist of manners, more in the tradition of Thackeray; her detailed delineation of society has been compared to Proust's. One critic called her an "authentic historian" of New York society, others believe her best novels do more than record: they give that society, as well as individuals caught in it, a life that will endure.

1862 Born Jan. 24 New York, N.Y.

1865-71 Studied in Europe

1885 Married Edward Wharton; divorced 1913

1899 Published *The Greater Inclination* (Short Stories)

1902 Published *The Valley of Decision*

1905 Published *The House of Mirth*

1907 Published *Madame de Treymes*

1911 Published *Ethan Frome*

1912 Published *The Reff*

1913 Published *The Custom of the Country*

1920 Published *The Age of Innocence*

1937 Died Aug. 11 St. Brice-sous-foret, France

EMMA WILLARD

Emma Willard believed that women could learn any subject that men could — a radical idea in America in 1820, and she proceeded to prove it. She devised new teaching techniques, wrote innovative textbooks, and founded the first school in America devoted to teaching women advanced courses in history, mathematics and science.

Emma Hart's father, a liberal who discussed Shakespeare and Locke with his children, encouraged Emma to read and to learn. She attended the community school and then taught there. A job teaching at the female academy in Middlebury, Vermont, proved challenging, but she left, after two years, to marry John Willard, a physician, and settled in Middlebury. Exposure to Middlebury College impressed upon her the scope of the curriculum of the traditional (*i.e.* male) college.

Financial problems beset the Willards and, in 1814, Emma Willard opened a school in her home. Gradually she mastered, and then taught, subjects actually considered at that time dangerous to a young woman's health (mathematics, languages). Middlebury Female Seminary soon prospered; the students (over 70) enjoyed — and passed — the new courses.

After her daring experiment in women's education had proved itself, Mrs. Willard put her "radical" ideas into a comprehensive plan, proposing an institution for women that offered courses in mathematics and science, etc., and was supported by the State. Her *Plan for Improving Female Education*, compact and tightly reasoned, offered a compelling argument for reform: "Education," she wrote — *in 1818* — "should seek to bring its subjects to the perfection of their moral, intellectual and physical nature...." A copy was sent to Governor DeWitt Clinton of New York and the New York legislature, resulting in a charter, but no funds, for a women's school in Waterford, N.Y.

Mrs. Willard moved her school to Waterford. Textbooks were scarce; in teaching solid geomoetry, she used cones and pyramids carved out of potatoes and turnips. in 1821 the Common Council of Troy (N.Y.) voted $4000 for a permanent building for her school: Troy Female Seminary opened that September with 90 students — the only women's school offering courses in history, mathematics and science.

At last Emma Willard could fully carry out her plan: she selected and developed courses, taught, hired assistants, established and maintained rules for students, and directed operations. Her husband served as business manager and school physician. She incorporated the materials and techniques developed for her geography and history courses into textbooks. The *Universal Geography* she co-authored and her history *Republic of America* won her recognition and royalties. Later, she published *Poems*; most famous — "Rocked in the Cradle of the Deep."

As the school grew (300 students in 1831), graduates carried her name — and teaching methods — to other States. In 1845 Mrs. Willard traveled 8000 miles through the South and West — a poised, articulate advocate of education for women.

Emma Willard did not join the first stirrings of the women's movement, but it is significant that, in 1819, she sent a copy of her plan to Thomas Jefferson, who strongly endorsed it. Both knew the liberating power of education.

EMMA WILLARD SCHOOL

1787	Born Feb. 23 Berlin, Conn.
1802-03	Attended Berlin Academy
1804-	Teacher, Berlin schools
1807-09	Teacher, Middlebury Female Academy
1809	Married Dr. John Willard; died 1825
1814	Founded Middlebury Female Seminary
1819	Founded Waterford Academy (N.Y.)
1819	Published *Plan for Improving Female Education*
1821	Founded Troy Female Seminary
1822	Published *Universal Geography* (Co-author)
1828	Published *Republic of America*
1838	Married Dr. Christopher Yates; divorced 1843
1870	Died Apr. 15 Troy, N.Y.

FRANCES WILLARD

As leader of the temperance movement in America in the late 19th century, Frances Willard fought for a wide range of social reforms — labor, prison, welfare, women suffrage — as well as temperance. In her handbook *Do Everything* she declared; "Every question of practical philanthropy or reform has its temperance aspect, and with that we are to deal."

Raised on the frontier in Wisconsin Territory, Frances grew up a spirited, independent tomboy. After college she taught at her alma mater and other schools and was head of the Genessee Wesleyan Seminary in Lima, N.Y. For two years she traveled through Europe and the Middle East with Kate Jackson, a wealthy friend, writing weekly articles for her home newspaper. After her return, she was appointed president of the new Evanston College for Ladies — the first woman president of an American college. When the college was absorbed by Northwestern, she became dean of women. After one year, friction with the university president led her to resign, making her, a well-known educator, available as the temperance movement began to gain momentum.

In one year (1874) Frances Willard went from head of the Chicago Women's Christian Temperance Union to corresponding secretary of the National W.C.T.U. From the first she expressed interest in a number of reforms besides temperance. As president of the Illinois W.C.T.U., she organized a campaign to secure women the right to vote on liquor questions: a petition with over 100,000 signatures was submitted to the State legislature and, though it failed, the impressive showing brought local option to most Illinois towns. Such successes, plus her stirring oratory at conventions, won her the presidency of the National W.C.T.U.

The new president's speaking tours brought in new members in State after State; under her direction the Union became more active in community affairs, obtaining the support of other reform groups and organized religion, and the annual convention became a spectacular, well-managed event attracting national attention. She re-organized the Union, establishing separate department for each area of reform — temperance, suffrage, welfare, etc.; in 1889 thirty-nine departments were working for legislation through education and lobbying. Her concern about international drug traffic led to the formation of the World's W.C.T.U. — with Miss Willard as first president.

Frances Willard became directly involved in other causes. She was active in the American Woman Suffrage Association, helped form the International Council of Women and the General Federation of Women's Clubs, and served as president of the National Council of Women and vice-president of the Universal Peace Union.

To win support for temperance — and suffrage, she brought the W.C.T.U. into American politics. She organized the Home-Protection Party, dedicated to temperance and suffrage, then merged with the Prohibition Party; her attempt to become part of the Populist Party failed, but in this as in her twenty years of W.C.T.U. leadership, she succeeded in stimulating national interest in temperance and suffrage and in introducing a generation of women seeking reforms to the American political system.

BY GEORGE RAPP

NATIONAL PORTRAIT GALLERY
SMITHSONIAN INSTITUTION

1839 Born Sep. 28 Churchville, N.Y.

1859 Graduated from North Western Female College, Evanston, Ill.

1862 Teacher, North Western Female College

1863-64 Teacher, Pittsburgh Female College

1864 Published *Nineteen Beautiful Years*

1866-67 Preceptress, Genessee Wesleyan Seminary, Lima, N.Y.

1871-73 President, Evanston College for Ladies

1873-74 Dean of Women, Northwestern University

1873 Helped found Association for the Advancement of Women

1874 Secretary, Illinois Women's Christian Temperance Union

1874-77 Corresponding Secretary, National Women's Christian Temperance Union

1878-79 President, Illinois W.C.T.U.

1879-98 President, National W.C.T.U.

1888-90 President, National Council of Women

1891- President, World's W.C.T.U.

1895 Published *Do Everything*

1898 Died Feb. 17 New York, N.Y.

107

MILDRED "BABE" DIDRIKSON ZAHARIAS

"There is only one Babe Didrikson and there has never been another in her class," Grantland Rice wrote: she excelled in more sports than any other woman — and perhaps any man except Jim Thorpe. The statistics are awesome: between 1930 and 1932 she held five American, Olympic or world track records; in the 1932 Olympics she won two gold medals, set two world records; she was an All-American basketball player in 1930, 1931 and 1932, and led her team to a national championship. she struck out Dimaggio and others pitching in major league exhibition games, won tennis and diving championships in Texas, and, as an amateur and professional golfer, won eighty-two touraments.

In the dusty South End of Beaumont, Texas, young Mildred Didrikson discovered early that she could run faster and hit a baseball farther than most boys; she was a fierce competitor ready to challenge anyone. In high school she competed in six sports — and once scored 99 points in a basketball game. She left school in 1930 to work for Employers Casualty Co. and play on its basketball team, the Golden Cyclones, in the semi-professional industrial league. In one of her first games she scored 36 points, in her first year was named All-American. That year with the Cyclone track team at the national AAU meet she broke the world record in the javelin, baseball throw and broad jump. The sudden rush to national recognition gave the already cocky Babe (named after babe Ruth) further cause to swagger; she boasted shamelessly of her exploits, antagonized opponents and teammates.

Babe's greatest performance in a single day occurred at the 1932 AAU national meet in Evanston, Illinois. In three hours she won six gold medals and broke four world records — according to United Press, "the most amazing series of performances accomplished by any individual, male or female, in track and field history." Her feats at the Olympics that summer were almost an anticlimax, but they commanded more attention: at Dallas and Beaumont thousands welcomed the new national hero.

Grantland Rice encouraged Babe to try golf. She took lessons, practiced tirelessly and, in 1935, won her first tournament, the Texas Women's Amateur Championship. Branded a professional, she played exhibitions, then sat out three years to regain amateur standing. She began to win tournaments — the Western Open, the Texas Open; in 1945 the Associated Press named her Woman Athlete of the Year (also in 1932, 1946, 1947, 1950, 1954). In 1946 she began a string of consecutive victories unmatched in golf: seventeen straight tournaments (closest: Byron Nelson — eleven straight, 1945) — her most prestigious win, the British Women's Amateur Championship.

With no more worlds to conquer, Babe turned professional and, with five others, formed the Ladies' Professional Golf Association. The first three years she was top money winner; then in 1953 doctors discovered incurable cancer; prognosis: never play golf again. The next year she won her third U.S. Women's Open, by a record twelve strokes.

BABE DIDRIKSON ZAHARIAS FOUNDATON

1911   Born Jun. 26 Port Arthur, Tex.

1930,   All-American, Golden Cyclones
1931,   (Basketball)
1932

1932   Won two gold medals, Olympics
        (Track)

1935   Winner, Texas Women's Amateur
        Championship (Golf)

1938   Married George Zaharias

1940   Winner, Western Open

1947   Winner, British Women's Amateur
        Championship (First American)

1948   Co-founder, Ladies' Professional Golf
        Association

1950   Named Woman Athlete of
        Half-Century

1954   Winner, U.S. Women's Open (Third
        Time)

1956   Died Sep. 27 Galveston, Tex.

Acknowledgements

For assistance in obtaining the portraits, I am indebted to:

Ms. Linda Neumaier & Ms. Susan Embree, National Portrait Gallery
Ms. Susan Boone, Women's History Archives, Smith College Archivist,
Mr. John Lancaster, Archivist, Amherst College Library
Mr. Franklin Riehlman, Photographic Library, Metropolitan
   Museum of Art
Ms. Sara Beckner, Oakland Museum
Mr. Mark Renovitch, Archivist, Franklin D. Roosevelt Library
Mr. Paul Palmer, Curator, Columbia University Library
Mr. Guy McElroy, Curator, Bethune Museum & Archives
Mr. Daniel Meyer, University of Chicago Library
Ms. Elizabeth Shenton, Schlesinger Library, Radcliffe College
Sister Aloysia, Archivist, St. Joseph's Provincial House
Mr. David Schoonover and Steven Jones, Yale University Library
Ms. Elaine Trehub, Librarian, Mount Holyoke College
Ms. Roseanne Cinnamond, National Woman's Party
Ms. Marilyn Marcus, Free-lance editor, New York City
Ms. Courty Hoyt, Life Pictures Service
Ms. Kay Beasley, Archivist, Vanderbilt University Library

For Assistance and advice, I am indebted to:

The members of the Advisory Group: Ms. Edith Mayo,
Dr. Evelyn Pugh and Ms. Sara Pritchard
Mrs. Caro Taylor, Mr. Larry Cody, and Mrs. Kathy Leonard of the Olney Library, and
Miss Estelle Alexander of the Reference Service of Montgomery County Library System
Mr. James Cavender of Pittsburg, Pa., graphics designer
Miss Mary C. Baker of Baltimore, who provided editorial assistance
Mrs. Linda Monds of R.R. Donnelley & Sons
Mrs. Shirley Kessel, Librarian, Mining Congress
Ms. Brenda Lee Mines of Baltimore
Ms. Sherri Ferritto of Graphica, Inc.
and members of my family —
my son, Nicholas, theatrical manager — an invaluable, resourceful assistant;
my daughter, Liza Wilson Bernard, career counselor, University of Pennsylvania — a sound critic;
Mr. Thomas Bernard, photographer, Venturi & Rauch — a perceptive photographic critic; and
my wife, Mary Jo, of the Cricket Bookshop in Ashton, Maryland — who offered wise criticism
and endless support.

Vincent Wilson, Jr. taught at several colleges and then served as a writer, editor and historian with the U.S. Government. Other books in this series, begun in 1962, include *The Book of the Presidents, The Book of the Founding Fathers, The Book of the States,* and *The Book of Great American Documents.* The latter two were selected for awards by the Freedoms Foundation at Valley Forge. A native of Cleveland, Mr. Wilson studied at Cleveland's University School and at Georgetown, Arizona State, Claremont and Harvard.

To order additional copies of

The Book of Distinguished American Women ($4.50)

Or copies of our other publications:

The Book of the Presidents ($3.50)
The Book of Great American Documents ($3.50)
The Book of the States ($3.00)
The Book of the Founding Fathers ($2.00)

(Add 75¢ per copy for postage and handling)

Send check or money order to:

Order Dept.
American History Research Associates
P.O. Box 140
Brookeville, Maryland 20833